BRITAIN
by Bike

FOREWORD BY CLARE BALDING

JANE EASTOE

BRITAIN *by Bike*

A TWO-WHEELED
ODYSSEY AROUND
BRITAIN

BATSFORD

First published in the United Kingdom in 2010 by
Batsford
10 Southcombe Street
London
W14 0RA

An imprint of Anova Books Company Ltd

Text by Jane Eastoe

Produced in association with Lion Television Ltd,
26 Paddenswick Road, London W6 0UB

ISBN: 9781906388713

A CIP catalogue record for this book is available from the British Library.

16 15 14 13 12 11 10
10 9 8 7 6 5 4 3 2 1

Consultant on cycle routes: Mark Jarman

Reproduction by Mission Productions Ltd, Hong Kong
Printed and bound by Butler Tanner & Dennis, Frome, UK

This book can be ordered direct from the publisher at the website www.anovabooks.com

CONTENTS

FOREWORD

The first Christmas present I remember wanting so badly that it hurt was a bicycle. Only a few years ago, I asked for a bicycle again and was transported back to my childhood years. There is something wonderfully liberating about travelling around the country on a bike, covering the miles while feeling everything around – the wind, the rain, the sunshine, the smell of freshly cut grass or the less attractive odour of silage.

Using Harold Briercliffe's touring guides from the 1940s as my starting point, I took Harold's own bicycle all over the UK. It was an adventure that allowed me to fall in love all over again with the rich variety of this country's landscape. I shall never forget the mist rising off Loch Duich like steam, the mountains known as the Five Sisters reflected in the water or the solitary hot-air balloon that floated over the Vale of Evesham as I stood on top of Broadway Tower admiring the 360° view of thirteen different counties.

Travelling on a bicycle allowed me to cover the ground while giving me time to stop and stare, to soak up the views and to meet people who had a tale to tell. I came across other cyclists making journeys of their own, and immediately felt that I was part of a community where we all shared a passion. They would ask me about Harold's bike as I admired, with a touch of envy, their 26-gear wonder machines with wide tyres and gel-injected saddles. I felt as if I had joined a big, happy team who would swap tips, exchange stories and offer help in a crisis.

I journeyed past the stone walls and yellow cottages of Gloucestershire, through the seaside town of Ventnor on the Isle of Wight, along the heather-clad hilltops of North Devon down into the town of Ilfracombe, through the Welsh valleys, the Yorkshire Dales and the Highland glens.

For every exhausting, painful climb there was the reward of flying down the hill, the wind rushing past my ears and sheep wondering who the crazy woman was, shouting 'Whoopee!' That childlike thrill that I first had on a bicycle was rediscovered and I felt a blast of pure pleasure, mixed with adrenaline that made me want to laugh. It was glorious, invigorating, challenging and unforgettable. Harold Briercliffe was my inspiration and I hope that this book may be yours.

CLARE BALDING

INTRODUCTION

Sixty years ago, the extraordinary Harold Briercliffe wrote a series of books about his great passion: bicycle touring. Now largely forgotten, these overlooked classics were the culmination of an epic journey across Britain. Briercliffe cycled across the country he loved, reporting on major landmarks and forgotten vistas. His six *Cycle Touring Guides*, published between 1947 and 1950, covered Britain region by region, faithfully recording the ever-changing landscape and highlighting the progressive alterations in our way of life.

No one becomes familiar with a country by driving through it at high speed. Cycling allows us to develop an intimate and in-depth understanding of our landscape, to be familiar with its changes, across the seasons, across county boundaries and from country to country. Everything is magnified. The small villages that car drivers bypass boast a diverting geographic feature or historical footnote just crying out to be explored. Breaks for cream teas, pints of beer, or paper cornets of fish and chips are no longer guilty pleasures, but essential pit stops that fuel your journey. Great sweeping vistas can be examined in detail; changes in gradient and climate are exhilarating physical experiences.

This is an unfamiliar and unashamedly old-fashioned experience. No queuing, no road rage, no being hustled along. Cycle tourers can travel where they please, detour as they fancy and experience real freedom and tranquility in the process. The shared camaraderie of touring, whether with friends or family, can create life-long golden memories. Touring is as much about discovering the land, exploring and learning as it is about cycling. Briercliffe was well aware of this and he was forever urging his readers to abandon their bicycles to climb up to some remote beauty spot, to sit on the beach or enjoy a local delicacy.

Harold was also not averse to some serious physical challenges, as well as the gentle touring routes. He writes about the 'rough stuff', cycling in mountainous regions on week-long tours. He also commends the fetish of pass-storming: the enthusiastic (read young and fit) pass-stormer pedals up rough mountain tracks, continuing on foot, bicycle on back, when the going gets too tough and then tearing down the far side. However, he also advocates hopping on trains, bicycle stashed in the guard's van, if the mood takes you.

Harold Briercliffe's *Cycle Touring Guides* divided the country into six regions: The Scottish Highlands, Northern England, The Midlands, Wales, Southern England and South-West England. Rather curiously he seemed to overlook the cycle-friendly flatlands of Eastern England, which were perhaps not challenging enough for his adventurous spirit. In each guide he took his readers on a selection of tours, offering his own personal and sometimes waspish critique of the area. As well as major tourist attractions he draws our attention to quirky and diverting features, creating a distinct snapshot of post-war Britain, one that might be assumed to have changed beyond all recognition. In fact, this is not so.

Many of Harold's favourite routes are as charming today as they ever were. And, although there is a greater volume of traffic on the roads, in many ways cycling has become easier. 'The road between Penzance and Land's End on a July day has as many buses and cars as Piccadilly', complains Harold. The journey today can be undertaken on designated cycle routes on quiet country roads that most motorists miss. Our cycling experience is also being transformed by the National Cycle Network, a comprehensive web of safe and attractive routes throughout the UK, some 12,000 miles (19,300km) exist to date, one third of which are on traffic-free routes. Signposted routes run from John o' Groats to Land's End, from east to west, through beauty spots and cities, and link coast to coast. The question today isn't why are you cycling, but why aren't you?

It is apparent that despite the ravages of time and the march of progress, our land and seascapes are remarkably unchanged. Historic remains and topographic features have been preserved, often because of the determination of committed locals. Moreover, it is a dynamic environment and all manner of new attractions have sprung up, from The Angel of the North in Gateshead to a secret nuclear bunker in Kelvedon Hatch in Essex, only decommissioned in 1992.

Britain by Bike picks up where Harold's *Cycling Touring Guides* left off, letting us discover where pedal power can take us in today's Britain. We explore the country region by region, including the somewhat neglected eastern counties, enjoying breathtaking scenery, delighting in regional features and revelling in historical highlights ancient and modern. Cycle-friendly routes are listed and in each area we detail two favourite routes for readers to follow. Harold is a companion throughout and his perspective from the 1940s provides a fascinating account.

You will not get to know the country by reading this book. Only by wobbling off into the sunset on two wheels, book in saddle bag, will you discover the forgotten joy of touring for yourself.

THE HISTORY OF CYCLING

'Life is like riding a bicycle. To keep your balance you must keep moving.' Albert Einstein

The bicycle is a comparatively recent invention, given that the first human-powered machine was built by the Venetian Giovanni Fontana back in 1418. Admittedly it had four wheels and was pulled by a rope, but the concept was under consideration. The first primitive two-wheeled, man-powered machine appeared in 1817 when a German inventor, Baron Karl von Drais, created the *Laufmaschine*, a running machine, to help him to move around at greater speed. This wooden contraption had two in-line wheels, which the rider straddled, propelling himself along by foot. It was enormously popular and was lauded by the dandies of the day. In England, where it was known as the 'hobby-horse', one enthusiast raced against a four-horse coach to Brighton on his running machine and beat it by half an hour – though the length of the actual ride is unknown. Modern manufacturers have revisited the design to help young children learn to balance on two wheels, propelling themselves forwards by foot without the complication of pedalling.

It must be acknowledged, however, that a design for a bicycle was found some three hundred years earlier among the manuscripts of Leonardo da Vinci. These are thought to date from his studio in the 1490s and are believed to be the work of a pupil, although others argue that the drawing is a hoax. The design, which lacks any apparent means of steering, is not sophisticated but, if genuine, it shows that the technological capabilities for the bicycle were understood long before von Drais turned the dream into a reality.

EARLY BICYCLE DESIGNS

After 1817 the depth of enthusiasm for two-wheeled, human-powered machines and the lure of handsome profits encouraged amateur mechanics to experiment with the concept. Some extraordinary flights of design fancy emerged utilizing, one, two, three and four wheels. These might be powered by hand cranking or treadle drives for the foot with steering at the back or the front. In 1839 a blacksmith, Kirkpatrick Macmillan, designed and made a machine that local newspapers reported allowed him to travel the 70 miles from his home near Dumfries to Glasgow in five hours – an astonishing speed in its day. In 1842 Alexandre Lefèbvre created a more sophisticated version of Macmillan's machine. He never achieved fame for his designs, but one example survived and it is believed to be the oldest existing bicycle in the world.

You have heard of old Pegasus flying no doubt
But our Hobbies now Beat him good luck
For when you are tired of Riding about
You may carry your Horse on your Back

· THE · PEDESTRIAN · HOBBIES · or the Difference of going Up and Down Hill is Cheapside

ABOVE: The mania for riding the hobby was adored by caricaturists, who remorselessly poked fun at the gentleman of leisure who scooted around the parks and streets of London in their hundreds.
PAGE 10: Cycling in Hyde Park in 1900. Cycling in the park was permitted only in 1895.

In 1865 the term 'velocipede', literally meaning fast foot, became commonly used to describe wooden, wheeled machines that had pedals attached to the front wheel. There is some considerable dispute over quite who first attached the cranks, whether it was the aforementioned Lefèbvre, who used rear-wheel cranks, or Ernest Michaux or Pierre Lallemont, who used front-wheel cranks and who filed the earliest patent for the pedal bicycle.

BRITISH BONESHAKERS

In the UK velocipedes acquired the moniker 'boneshaker' because they were so uncomfortable to ride over cobbled streets. Comfort was in fact a major drawback to early cycling; road surfaces were poor and many enthusiasts concentrated on cycling in specially built arenas. The riding of the velocipede was initially limited to the wealthy and upper classes and was regarded as a social accomplishment to be developed along with dancing and riding. Velocipedes served a more useful purpose for messenger boys, while scantily clad ladies used them for entertainment in music halls and circuses by performing acrobatics on them. The sport was dominated by men but women were very much interested in the velocipede, and indeed, some doctors recommended it as a gentle form of exercise somewhat more modest than dancing in a tight corset in the arms of an ardent suitor.

The velocipede was not swift, but there was a growing interest in its potential for touring. In 1869 two men from the Liverpool Velocipede Club rode from Liverpool to London in just three days; the *Times* reported that the machines caused great excitement in the villages they passed through. Velocipedes were also a huge hit with public schoolboys – they were banned by Eton College, however, for they enabled boys to pass out of bounds in a flash.

Parks and arenas were packed with adults trying to master the precarious art of cycling. H.G. Wells observed: 'To ride a bicycle properly is very like a love affair; chiefly it is a matter of faith. Believe you can do it and the thing is done, doubt, and for the life of you, you cannot.' Mark Twain declared: 'Get a bicycle. You will not regret it, if you live.' Small boys were often employed to run alongside as a means of support.

THE PENNY FARTHING AND TRICYCLE

In 1869 the high-wheel bicycle, otherwise known as the penny farthing, was invented. It boasted a metal frame and a giant front wheel with spokes, the size of which was dictated by the inside-leg measurement of the rider. The advantage of this stately design was that it travelled further per revolution of the wheel and that it offered a more comfortable ride than the velocipede. The downside was the health and safety risk – the penny farthing was famously inclined to tip its rider forwards in a dramatic head-first dive. The braking mechanism was limited and hazardous, to say the least; back-pedalling could be utilized or a small, lever-operated brake could be employed – either, if misjudged, could cause the rider to come a cropper. The high-wheel bicycle was ridden almost exclusively by men – it was considered far too dangerous for women to attempt.

OPPOSITE: H.L. Cortis, noted cyclist of his day, is given a helping hand by his trainer to climb aboard his 59in (1.5m) 'Invincible' Ordinary, or penny farthing, in 1882.

THE CYCLISTS' TOURING CLUB

The Bicycle Touring Club was formed in the UK in 1878, and later renamed the Cyclists' Touring Club (CTC). It is said to be the oldest national tourism organization in the world. The CTC produced maps for cyclists and placed 'Danger' signs at the top of steep hills to alert cyclists to the steep gradient ahead – brakes being dangerously unreliable. In addition, seals of approval – cast-iron winged wheels – were left outside some hotels and restaurants to indicate that cyclists would be welcome in that establishment; a few still remain. The CTC campaigned for cycle access to parks and, in short, did everything possible to promote the concept of leisure cycling. Membership of the Cyclists' Touring Club rose dramatically between 1895 and 1899 from some 16,300 members to more than 60,000.

ABOVE: The members of Wood Green (Essex) Cycle Club pose for a group photograph in 1890, all neatly kitted out in knickerbockers and caps.

Tricycles were developed to offer a more stable and dignified option. Professional men such as doctors and clergymen, as well as women, favoured this alternative, which allowed them to retain their poise while revelling in the liberation and freedom the machine offered. Tandem tricycles ensured that women riders could be chaperoned at all times. The disadvantage was that tandem tricycles or 'Sociables', which allowed two riders to sit side by side, were expensive to buy and required a large storage space.

CYCLING CLUBS

Cycling clubs became popular and on Saturdays group runs out and about were planned – riding on the Sabbath was frowned upon by the Church of England.

These excursions were led by a club captain, equipped with a bugle to control his members. Trips were confined to the spring and summer months as roads were often too wet and muddy at other times of the year. We must be careful not to romanticize these days or imagine that the open road without motor vehicles was an entirely harmonious place; coach and cart drivers resented cyclists and were known to use a whip or to run cyclists off the road. Small boys were known to throw stones. Cycling in parties discouraged harassment and offered women protection. Cyclists returning home after dark travelled in groups, their bicycles bedecked with Chinese lanterns.

RIGHT: In summer, cycle clubs planned moonlight rides for its members, and riders festooned their machines with paper lanterns to celebrate the occasion and light their way, illustrated here in 1902.

THE ROVER SAFETY BICYCLE (PATENTED).

Safer than any Tricycle, faster and easier than any Bicycle ever made. Fitted with handles to turn for convenience in storing or shipping. Far and away the best hill-climber in the market.

MANUFACTURED BY

STARLEY & SUTTON,

METEOR WORKS, WEST ORCHARD, COVENTRY, ENGLAND.

Price Lists of "Meteor, "Rover," "Despatch," and "Sociable" Bicycle and Tricycles, and the "Coventry Chair," Illustrated, free on application.

ABOVE: An 1885 advertisement from Rover for the revolutionary safety bicycle, described here as 'faster and easier than any bicycle ever made' – and it probably was.

THE SAFETY BICYCLE

In 1884 John Kemp Starley invented the safety bike – the real father of the modern bicycle. The wheels were of equal or similar size, and a chain mechanism linked to the pedals drove the back wheel, leaving the front wheel free for smoother, easier steering. The design was safe enough for women and children to ride as well as men. Comfort was still an issue, however, although saddles were now sprung to minimize discomfort.

Of equal significance in the development of the bicycle was the invention of the pneumatic tyre in 1887 by John Boyd Dunlop, who came up with idea of fitting air-filled tyres to his son's tricycle. In 1891 in France, Edouard Michelin developed a detachable tubeless tyre and there was serious competition between the two companies as to whose tyres were the best. Efforts were made to put tyres on penny farthings but the idea did not take off.

The stable design of the safety bicycle and the cushioning properties of tyres transformed the practice of cycling, and by the 1890s its role as an efficient provider of transport for men, women and children was established. It is estimated that by 1896 there were one million bicycles in England and France, half a million in Germany and three million in the United States.

REVOLUTIONARY CYCLING

In Britain the bicycle was becoming more egalitarian. In 1892 an issue of the periodical *The Cyclist* identified clerks and shop assistants as a new force in the cycling fraternity. Cycling had social implications, too; a study undertaken in 1969 by P.J. Perry showed that marriages in rural Dorset to partners living a distance of 6 to 12 miles away increased from 3 per cent to 9 per cent between 1907 and 1916, a statistic that Perry attributed to the increased mobility of cyclists. The royal family showed consistent support for the bicycle over the decades; King Edward VII, George V, Edward VIII and George VI were all cyclists. In contrast, the upper classes diverted their attention to the automobile after their initial enthusiasm for cycling had waned.

While some doctors expressed concern about women participating in such 'vigorous' exercise as cycling, the notion that their reproductive organs might shake loose faded. Women's principal deterrent was in fact the matter of costume. How to look decent when cycling was the issue; the questions of the morality or social niceties of cycling were academic when women's clothes prevented them from climbing on bicycles in the first place.

ABOVE: The book *Fancy Cycling*, published in 1901, was devoted to teaching amateur riders the sorts of stunts and tricks teenagers do today.

It was American women who first took up the standard. In 1851, a Mrs Libby caused a scandal on a visit to the social reformers Amelia Bloomer and Elizabeth Stanton by wearing baggy harem pants. An early advocate of rational dress, Mrs Bloomer lauded the design of the garment that was later dubbed 'bloomers' in her honour. The look did not catch on, but they were adopted by a couple of women cyclists in the spring of 1893 and within two years they were commonly seen on female cyclists in the United States.

The advent of the safety bicycle in the mid-1880s encouraged women to be more adventurous. Cycling for women took off in the spring of 1895: society women championed the bicycle, albeit dressed in traditional clothing. The bicycle had become respectable. The American civil rights campaigner Susan B. Anthony said: 'Let me tell you what I think of bicycling. I think it has done more to emancipate women than anything else in the world. It gives women a feeling of freedom and self-reliance.'

THE RISE AND RISE OF THE BICYCLE

The speed of movement and the popularity of the safety bicycle meant that police forces and armies were drawn to it. Policemen on bicycles could, if sufficiently motivated, stop a runaway horse-drawn carriage. In 1883, proving that road rage is not a new phenomenon, Andrew Weiss massacred six cyclists

WOMEN'S FASHION
AND CYCLING

French women were racing on velocipedes as early as 1868; the amount of leg on show was considered scandalous. On the streets of Paris women were more decorous, but not averse to showing off a finely turned ankle. British women were more modest and desisted from riding penny farthings. The advent of the tricycle allowed women to cycle in relative safety, in everyday modest dress, with a chaperone beside them. Convention was thus not threatened and women learned that cycling was fun. Social reformers, such as Mrs King, Secretary of the Rational Dress Society, championed practical clothing for women. She railed against the stupidity of women tricyclists attempting to cycle in tight-waisted dresses with billowing skirts – indeed, newspapers regularly reported hideous cycling accidents caused by women's dresses. Nevertheless, women were generally not prepared to rock the boat, though there were some notable exceptions. In 1893, Tessie Reynolds rode from London to Brighton and back in just eight and a half hours wearing knickerbockers; her cycling achievement was ignored but her costume caused a storm of protest.

The Rational Dress Society did not recommend that women wore men's trousers for cycling, but instead they proposed the wearing of looser, divided skirts worn with long jackets. In 1895 the cycling press reported that women in 'Rational' dress were subjected to torrents of abuse. Lady Harberton adopted the style and was refused refreshments in a hotel in Ockham, Surrey, because of her unsuitable costume.

The real social reform in dress came during the First World War when simpler garments became more acceptable and sportswear filtered into everyday use. By 1916 women's skirt lengths had risen to mid-calf, trousers were worn for war work and women began to have their hair cut short. They were never to look back.

ABOVE: The term 'loose women' is said to come from female cyclists who loosened their corsets in order to ride. Here a young woman in divided skirts mounts a man's bicycle c.1896.

in Central Park, New York, by shooting them from the top of his wagon. By the late nineteenth century, bicycle touring was becoming popular in America, though this was clearly still a hazardous enterprise and many cyclists carried firearms. Sears and Roebuck marketed a collapsible 'bicycle rifle' that could be used either as a pistol or a rifle – a concept that gives the bicycle a rather more rakish and dangerous image than its clean-cut, eco-friendly one of today.

The bicycle was put to good use on the American Frontier and during the gold rush in Western Australia (1892–7). The clergy, sheepshearers and the post office relied on bicycles as transport. Bicycles even had military significance, being heavily employed in both the Boer War and the First World War.

RACING

From its earliest inception the bicycle has encouraged competitive racing, though initially it was considered sufficiently daring to break the speed limit –

ABOVE: Cycle races were hugely popular with the general public, but after numerous complaints from the police, the public and the press many were moved away from roads and into stadiums. This early twentieth-century illustration shows German cycle racers in action.

OPPOSITE: Track events made money for promoters and allowed the public to see their cycling heroes in action. This illustration shows a crowd enjoying a race meeting in 1914.

set at 10mph (16kph) in the UK in 1861. Six-day races were held at Madison Square Gardens in 1891. Pairs of riders worked as teams, each cycling 12 hours at a stretch on wooden tracks in an indoor arena. They were so popular that they spawned a rash of six-day races across the United States. At its peak in the 1920s, race events could attract some 20,000 spectators. Cycle racing was introduced to the Olympics as early as 1896, though it should be noted that there was no such event for women until 1958.

Velocipede racing was immensely popular in indoor arenas in Europe, but an interest in road racing was also developing, notably in France. City-to-city races were introduced: Paris to Rouen in 1869, Paris to Bordeaux and Paris–Brest–Paris races in 1891. The first Tour de France took place in 1903. The route, which changes annually, covers all manner of terrain and climactic extremes and is acknowledged to be the most gruelling endurance race. It is estimated that the Tour de France attracts around 30 million spectators in its home country – half of the population. Undoubtedly racing has driven many of the advances in bicycle design.

TOURING BY BICYCLE

The concept of touring by bicycle became a more practical reality for many after the First World War. The cost of bicycles had decreased and lightweight touring bicycles were advertised as a means of getting away from it all. Developments in gear systems, including the patenting of the very first *derailleur* gear system, made touring even easier. Furthermore, legislation in the 1930s limiting the number of working hours and introducing the concept of holidays with pay ensured that many more men and women escaped from the daily grind in factories, mills, shops and offices by hiking and cycling in the great outdoors. Moreover, women, who had worn trousers during the war, were happier to adopt the sensible sporting dress that cycling demanded. For many it was their very first experience of travel.

Cycling no longer held any social status, since most shops had delivery boys on bicycles – Sainsbury's had its own fleet, as did Wall's Ice Cream, which sold its wares via Stop-Me-and-Buy-One tricycles. Postmen, telegraph boys, chimney sweeps, window cleaners, indeed, tradesmen everywhere used them as transport. Figures from the 1930s indicate that in the UK there were some nine million regular cyclists compared to just two and a half million car drivers.

Cycling, however, fitted in with the outdoor movement that gained strength in the 1930s. Camping was popular, as was the new Youth Hostelling Movement, which started in Germany in 1912 and spread across the western world. Youth Hostels offered low-cost accommodation and their staff were knowledgeable about hiking and cycling in their area.

As late as 1939, bicycles were still an important form of transport. In the Second World War the Germans employed them as an effective means of moving troops. The Home Guard in the UK and the French Resistance famously relied on them, as did the British troops in the D-Day invasion. The Japanese managed to take Singapore with 35,000 troops – and a lot of bicycles.

BELOW: In the 1930s improved working conditions, with fewer working hours and paid holidays, encouraged working men and women to enjoy their free time exploring the countryside, often on two wheels.

THE BICYCLE
IN THE SECOND WORLD WAR

When Japan invaded China in 1937, it employed some 50,000 bicycle troops. Early in the Second World War, their southern campaign through Malaya, en route to capturing Singapore in 1941, was largely dependent on bicycle-mounted soldiers. In both efforts bicycles facilitated the quiet and flexible transport of thousands of troops who were then able to surprise and confuse the defending forces.

Allied use of the bicycle in the Second World War was more limited but included supplying folding bicycles to paratroopers and to messengers behind friendly lines. The term 'bomber bikes' came into use during this period, as US forces dropped bicycles out of planes to reach troops behind enemy lines.

Back in Britain bicycles were invaluable to the civilian population and the Home Front, especially with the rationing of fuel, which continued until 26 May 1950.

LEFT British soldiers from the Black Watch regiment patrol the south coast of England c. 1941.

ABOVE Allied commandos with their bicycles landing on the Anzio-Nettuno beachhead in 1944.

CAR VERSUS BICYCLE

Postwar Britain boasted around 12 million cyclists, but numbers declined rapidly. Many servicemen had learned to drive in the course of the war and wanted to utilize their newfound skill, but few could afford to buy a car. Even so, postwar transport policies in the UK favoured the motorist and little thought was given to the cyclist as the country was rebuilt. The Netherlands, in contrast, used the opportunity of postwar reconstruction to develop a network of cycle lanes to cover the entire country, with the result that the bicycle became the transport of choice in towns and cities. H.G. Wells would have approved, he proclaimed that: 'Cycle tracks will abound in Utopia.'

As prosperity grew in the late 1950s and early 1960s use of the bicycle slowly declined in favour of the car and, as the number of motorists increased, cycling correspondingly became more hazardous. In 1961 just three out of 10 households in the UK owned a car, but by the end of the twentieth century seven out of 10 households owned at least one car. Over the same period the number of households with two or more cars increased from 2 per cent to 28 per cent. There are now more than 10 times as many cars as there were in 1950.

It appeared that the bicycle might have had its day, but revolutionary new designs revitalized the old-fashioned image of the machine. In 1962 Alex Moulton created a small-wheeled bicycle with a new, improved suspension designed to take the pain out of riding on small wheels. The Moulton, essentially created for urban use, has been described as being as much of a style icon of its time as the mini car.

THE RISE OF THE BMX AND MOUNTAIN BIKE

In the late 1960s in the US a new form of cycling was established. Cross-country motorbike racing, or Motocross, became popular and in California teenagers started racing on dirt tracks on small-wheeled pedal bikes. The enthusiasm for the sport encouraged manufacturers to develop a new style of bike, the BMX (short for Bicycle Motocross), which allowed riders to perform stunts and tricks and to handle cross-country cycling and racing. The wheels were small – just 16–24in (40–60cm) in diameter and the frame was reinforced to allow for high jumps and wheel turns. Enthusiasm for the sport spread rapidly and the first world championships were held in 1982. The design transformed attitudes to cycling.

In the late 1970s Joe Breeze and Gary Fisher were early pioneers of the mountain bike, designed to allow off-road cycling and inspired by the landscapes around San Francisco. Mountain bikes are built to perform on rough terrain and to be durable enough to withstand extreme riding conditions. The bicycles have a larger range of gears to accommodate hill climbing and have wider, stronger tyres than road cycles.

Another factor in the resurrection of the bicycle was an increased awareness of the value of exercise in the 1970s, allied to the fitness boom of the 1980s. At the same time, cyclists began to push for more rights and more routes. In 1977, after 99 years of campaigning, the Cyclists' Touring Club (CTC) finally won free train carriage for bicycles in the UK – with some exceptions, notably tandems. Campaigns today aim to improve the road environment for cyclists and to double the number of cyclists, arguing that there is safety in numbers. Financial and practical incentives help, too; the oil crisis of 1973 has been credited with increasing the number of cyclists on the roads right across Europe, and when the Mayor of London introduced the Congestion Charge in London in 2003, the number of cyclists increased by an extremely impressive 24 per cent, while the number of cars dropped by a whopping 70,000 per day.

Contemporary bicycles are essentially hybrids of mountain bikes and road bicycles. They are fast and light, with broad tyres for comfort, load-bearing and for flexibility over a range of surfaces. Inspiration has been drawn from the motor and aeronautical industries and new materials include aluminium, titanium, carbon fibre, fibreglass, plastic and the eco-friendly bamboo.

The only real challenge to the classic bicycle design over the decades has been that of the two- or three-wheeled recumbent machine, where the rider lies back with his or her legs stretched out straight in front. The pedals, which drive the rear wheel, are sited above the front wheel. The design, which was first developed in 1934, encountered much resistance. It was banned from races because it could reach superior speeds; a recumbent bike holds the human-powered speed record of 82mph (132kph) on level ground. Enthusiasts argue that this is the bicycle of the future: fast and efficient. The disadvantage is that recumbents are currently less easy to use in adverse weather conditions and there are safety concerns, users being less visible on the lower-slung design.

Cycling today is seen as healthy, practical, environmentally friendly and easy on the pocket. London has witnessed a 107 per cent increase in cycling since 2000. Recreational cycling has similarly become a more attractive option, with an

ABOVE: 'Just as the ideal of classic Greek culture was the perfect harmony of mind and body, so a human and a bicycle are the perfect synthesis of body and machine.' Here a female mountain biker illustrates cycle writer Richard Ballantine's quote.

increasing number of scenic traffic-free routes and beautiful, approved off-road trails. Cycling currently has a buzz about it that it has lacked for decades; these near-perfect machines, with no downside, will always have a place.

PRACTICAL ADVICE ON CYCLING

'Marriage is a wonderful invention, but then again so is a bicycle repair kit.' **Billy Connolly**

The form of the bicycle is so near perfect that its design has changed but little over the last hundred years. While the technology and component parts have evolved to offer a smother, faster and safer ride, the basic principle remains the same: the rotary mechanism of the human leg is translated into smooth travel. The energy a cyclist expends in relation to their weight and the distance travelled is believed to make them the most efficient of all moving animals and machines; in theory, 99 per cent of the energy transmitted by the cyclist into the pedals is delivered into the wheels. A cyclist travelling at relatively low speeds (10-15mph/16–24kph) uses only the energy required to walk. In towns and villages cyclists are required not to exceed the speed limit of 20–30mph (32–48kph), which, given the right conditions, is surprisingly easy to do.

SAFE CYCLING

A cyclist is considered to be the operator of a vehicle and must abide by legal requirements; in most western countries cycles must be roadworthy, they must have a rear reflector, front and rear lights from dusk, a bell and, in some countries (not yet including the UK), it is compulsory that a helmet is worn.

TYPES OF BICYCLE: ROAD, MOUNTAIN AND HYBRID

The most important considerations in any bicycle purchase are, first, that it fits its function – a touring bicycle is different to one that is used for road racing – and secondly, that it is the correct fit for you, the rider. Road bikes are designed for speed; they are light, agile machines with large wheels and narrow tyres generally used for racing and fitness. Mountain bikes are designed for riding off-road; they are strong with good suspension and manoeuvrability, and they offer a comfortable ride which makes them popular with commuters.

Hybrid designs combine the speed of the road bike and strength of the mountain bike; they have larger wheels and the frame and suspension of a mountain bike. These popular, versatile bikes can be used for touring and commuting. Street bikes are one step down from road bikes; they are fast, large-wheeled machines with the upright riding position of a mountain bike and are favoured by commuters who want to build up speed. City bikes are pared-down

TOP: A man's mountain bike has smaller wheels with thicker tyres to give comfort, acceleration and strength. **ABOVE:** The ladies' hybrid bike is a mix of a road bike and a mountain bike to combine speed and durability.

mountain bikes designed for urban use. Committed tourers should consider the purchase of a special machine. Touring bicycles are strong – they can take plenty of luggage and still give you a comfortable ride, but they can also be used for commuting and general use.

THE RIGHT-SIZE BIKE

Finding the right fit is a fiendishly complex business with alarming swerves in measurements from imperial to metric and all manner of complex mathematical calculations – such as multiplying by 109 per cent (to obtain the saddle-top-to-pedal distance). However, it is important to take the trouble to ensure that your bicycle is a perfect fit. The relative positions of hands, feet and seat will ensure that you have a comfortable ride and that you can deliver power to the pedals at maximum efficiency. There are infinite variables of fit that need to be fine tuned. In the simplest terms the bicycle must be the right height for your leg length in order to achieve the correct stand-over height when straddling the bicycle, with your bottom just touching the saddle. There should be clearance between your crotch and the top tube, or crossbar, of 1.5–2in (3.8–5cm) for a road bike and 4in (10cm) for a mountain bike.

You will need to ensure that your seat is in the correct position – straight – and that you can fully extend your leg when pedalling. The reach to the handlebars should be comfortable, neither too hunched up nor too extended, and it should be easy to reach the brakes. Further fine-tuning can be undertaken to create the perfect bike for your build – the length of the handlebar stem and the width of the handlebars can be altered if required. For expert advice the best place to visit is a specialized cycle shop, where experts can help you manoeuvre your way through the minutiae of bicycle fit. If you are working with an old bike you may be able to make it fit better by changing the handlebars, handlebar stem and seat post.

If you are planning to use a bicycle for touring it must be comfortable. If you are travelling daily it is important that neither your back nor your bottom is going to be punished. It should be possible to sit in an

LEFT: A 1940s advert for Royal Enfield Bicycles. Although mostly known for its motorcycles, the Enfield company was set up in 1893 to manufacture bicycles, which it continued to do into the twentieth century.

upright position and take in the view without straining your neck or back, or taking too much weight on your wrists; the height, reach and angle of your handlebars can all be altered. The hands need to be protected – a choice of grips can be helpful, and adding padded tape to the handlebars for extra cushioning and wearing cycling gloves will make a difference.

CYCLE HELMETS

Cycle helmets are to be recommended, though in the UK the wearing of helmets is not mandatory. They are designed to protect your head if you fall off your bicycle and not against impact from a moving vehicle. Cycling is an aerobic activity, so helmets are vented to allow ventilation. A good fit is crucial – a loose helmet will simply fall off in an accident. Helmets come in a range of sizes for both children and adults, and they are sized small, medium and large within each group. The helmet should sit level on your head and there should be one or two finger widths between the helmet brim and the eyebrow. The strap should sit at the back of the jaw against the throat and should be sufficiently tight so that the helmet does not wobble – you should not be able to get more than one finger in between the throat and the strap. It should not be uncomfortably snug, but nor should you be able to pull it off when the strap is fastened. Don't buy any old helmet; make sure it complies with European safety standards or, if it is from a country where helmet-wearing is compulsory, that it fulfils the requirements of that country.

ABOVE: A cycle helmet is an important safety consideration; serious cyclists always wear them for good reason.

LIGHT THE WAY

Cyclists are legally required to use lights when it is dark. It is sheer lunacy not to use them, for without lights you are virtually invisible to motorists. Lights are used to enable you to see and, perhaps more importantly, to ensure that you can be seen by other road users. In towns we are used to street lighting, but when you are touring, dusk can fall suddenly and a good bicycle light with a strong front beam will keep you on the straight and narrow. This will also alert other drivers to your presence at road junctions. You are required by law to have a rear reflector as well as a red rear light. The intensity of light on offer varies, and it is important to select a type that suits your requirements – a feeble front light may be adequate under street lighting, but it won't cut the mustard on an unlit cycle track.

ABOVE: Based originally in Birmingham where it was established in 1872, Lucas provided lamps for cars and ships, and also acetylene lamps for bicycles.

There are plenty of lights on the market, ranging from the standard battery-operated lights to rechargeable battery-operated lights. High-power rechargeable headlights, such as halogen and HID (High Intensity Discharge), are more expensive but will offer savings in the long run. Halogen lights project an adjustable cone of light; they are reliable and very bright, suitable for off-road use, but can dazzle other road users. HID lights are some of the brightest lights on the market; they are expensive and are designed for serious off-road use. LED (Light-Emitting Diodes) lights offer low-energy consumption and a long life; they improve visibility, so are useful for cyclists who do a lot of night travelling. Flashing LEDs are legal in the UK provided that they emit a steady pulse. All these varieties require no wiring and are also easily detachable.

Dynamos offer permanent lighting solutions so suit many cyclists very well. They won't fail you when batteries expire and they won't get stolen or lost because they are wired into place. They are a little more expensive to purchase, but if you cycle at night regularly they will repay your initial investment. Tyre-driven dynamos need to be carefully installed – you do not want to cause undue wear and tear to your tyre wall. The disadvantage is that if you cycle very slowly they can go out and the dynamo can slip and leave you without a light. Hub dynamos are built into the wheel, which entails labour costs, and they are heavier than tyre dynamos; however, they are extremely efficient, do not wear the tyre and, blessedly, are silent. Take care to lock the wheel onto which the hub dynamo is built – or it might be stolen!

High-visibility clothing, whether jacket, tabard, strip or band, are as much a part of improving your visibility to other road users as your lights and should be worn day and night.

LOCKS

Approximately half a million bicycles are stolen in the UK each year. Most thefts are opportunistic, so leaving your bicycle alone for a moment while you nip into a shop is not a good idea. Leaving it left unlocked for any length of time is insanity. There is a broad range of locks on the market; you get what you pay for. Some locks are very good indeed and may secure you a reduction in your insurance premium, indeed, some insurance companies insist on specific brands of locks as

ABOVE: Bicycle locks don't necessarily prevent theft, but without them you can guarantee your bicycle will go AWOL. Here is a sample of the different locks available.

part of their policy. A general rule of thumb is to spend 10 per cent of the total cost of your bicycle on its security system. All security systems can be broken by a determined thief, but the better your system the more likely they are not to bother.

D-Locks are strong, rigid tubes of steel that form a D-shape. They enfold one wheel, the frame and the anchor and leave very little room for thieves to utilize leverage devices, but they don't fit around large anchor points, which can be a disadvantage. Always secure the D-lock with the lock facing downwards – this stops thieves from pouring glue into it, a technique they employ to prevent you removing it, thus buying themselves more time for the theft. D-locks are heavy, but you can buy a mounting bracket so the device can be attached to the bicycle as you ride. Thick chain locks and padlocks are also strong and effective, but they are heavy. Cable locks are not quite as efficient; basically, the thinner the cable, the easier it will be to cut through. Cable locks have the advantage of being long enough to fit around all sizes of anchor, however – indeed, it is often possible to include both wheels and the frame within the loop. Thinner cable locks can be cut with relative ease, but they are very useful in conjunction with other locking systems: secure one wheel and the main frame with a D-lock, then secure the other wheel to the frame with a cable lock.

Loop locks are attached to your bicycle frame and when you are going to leave it you pull the locking bar around and through the wheel to meet the other side of the lock. This is not a very secure method, as it simply prevents someone from riding the bicycle away; it isn't anchored to an immovable object but is very useful if you are just stopping for a few moments. Some police forces use it and on the continent it is often fitted to bikes as standard.

It is always worth having your bicycle security marked – that way, if it is stolen, you increase your chances of it being returned to you. It can also make it harder to sell on, so an unmarked bicycle may be of more interest to the thief than a security-marked one.

If you are looking for guidance there is an accreditation scheme, Sold Secure, which awards locks three grades; bronze (the lowest), silver and gold, according to how well they are able to withstand a prescribed attack. The Sold Secure logo on packaging will indicate that the product has been assessed and accredited. A final word of advice – always chain your bike to something tall, immovable and solid. The lock is useless if the bicycle and lock can simply be lifted over and off the anchor point. Always try to leave it somewhere busy and well lit, rather than a dark alley.

REPAIRS AND MAINTENANCE

No cyclist should be without the tools to repair their bicycle when a problem occurs. First and most important is a bicycle pump. You may not have a puncture – your tyre may simply need a little more air – but if your tyres are soft you are more vulnerable to a puncture, so it is important to keep them pumped up good and hard. There is a range of designs available; most are small and portable and can be mounted on the bicycle frame. Mountain bikes and road bikes can require different fittings – some pumps have adjustable fits that are suitable for all bike valves. Floor pumps are fine for home use but no good for touring, when the classic frame pump or a CO^2 pump will be your best choice.

 The other basic piece of non-negotiable equipment is a puncture-repair kit. This should include a spare inner tube, a pair of tyre levers and a patch kit. Make sure that your inner tube – the circular rubber tube that sits inside your bicycle tyre – is precisely the right diameter and width for your size and type of wheel. You can tell what size is required by looking at the wall of your tyre.

ABOVE: A 1930s hero helps two girls mend a puncture on the road. Fixing a puncture, however, is a skill that can easily be learnt (see pages 40–41) and there's no need to wait for a helping hand.

REPAIRING
A PUNCTURE

I f you have never done this, be reassured, it is a very simple process – a tyre can be changed in about fifteen minutes with a little practice. First, inspect the tyre to see if you can see what has caused the puncture and where it is located – it's easiest to do this if you first turn the bicycle upside down. There is no point repairing the inner tube if the nail that caused the damage is still sticking into the tyre. If you are very lucky and can see the cause and it is located well away from the valve, you may be able to repair the puncture without removing the whole wheel. You can simply ease out the affected area of inner tube using the method described below instead of removing the whole wheel. However, assuming the wheel has to come off, begin by putting the bicycle into its highest gear (on to the smallest rear cog) before you start; this gives a little slack on the chain and makes it easier to put the rear wheel back on. First release the wheel, either using the wheel-release levers or by unscrewing the nuts with a spanner. Release the brakes by pinching them together and lifting the cable out, then pull the upper *derailleur* pulley back and lift the wheel out.

Remove the cap from the inner-tube valve and remove the valve nut – put them somewhere safe. Place the thin end of the tyre levers between the tyre and the rim. Pry both levers; this action will pop the tyre over the rim – it's easiest if you start at the

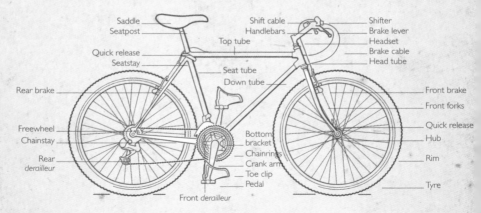

opposite side of the wheel to the valve instead of close to it. Loosen the tyre on one side only, all the way around. You can then remove the inner tube; the valve stem may need a little gentle persuasion. Feel the inside of the tyre carefully to check further whether anything sharp remains. Don't skip this step or you may end up dealing with another puncture a few miles down the road.

Either insert the spare inner tube or deal with the puncture on the spot. If you don't know where the puncture is, pump the tyre up and listen for a hissing noise. If it won't inflate at all, it may well be beyond repair. If you have access to still water you can put water on the tyre, or pop sections of the pumped-up inner tube in a pond or a basin and see where bubbles come out. As soon as you have found the puncture, mark the hole with chalk from the repair kit. The inner tube must be clean and dry before you start. Roughen a good-sized area around the puncture with a piece of sandpaper – don't be too rough. Next cover the area around the puncture with glue – ensure that the glued area is larger than the patch you intend to use. This ensures that the patch can fully bond to the inner tube.

When the glue is tacky, peel the backing off the patch, apply it to the puncture, press it on firmly and hold it tightly in place for a minute. Leave the top cover on the patch until you can be confident that the glue has set. When the patch is securely in place, remove the top cover. Dust any areas of excess glue with your chalk to stop it sticking to the tyre. Inflate the tube to ensure the puncture is fully repaired. Sometimes you may find a second puncture or that the valve is faulty.

The inner tube should be only partially inflated when being replaced. Put it back under the tyre starting with the valve; take care not to get it twisted. Use your hands to hook the tyre beading back out on to the rim, again starting with the valve. This can be harder with mountain bikes and sometimes one has to risk using tyre levers to start with. Getting the last section of tyre over the rim is always a little problematic – don't use the tyre levers here because you can create pinch flats (a hole in the inner tube); instead roll the tyre out on to the rim. Pinch the walls of the tyre and check carefully all the way around to ensure that the inner tube isn't trapped. If the inner tube is caught between the rim and tyre bead then you will quickly find you have a very explosive puncture. Replace the valve nut and inflate the tyre.

Pull the chain out and refit the wheel, fasten the levers or replace and tighten the bolts. Finally, re-connect the brakes. When the puncture is repaired, hop on the bicycle and move off slowly to check that the tyre and wheel is working properly; check your brakes, too.

Every cyclist should carry a multi-tool kit – even if you are a hopeless mechanic you must have the equipment to attempt a repair if something goes awry on an isolated country road. Even if it is beyond your skills, someone else may be able to advise or assist. A multi-tool kit includes such items as a screwdriver, wrenches, Allen keys, box spanners, tyre levers, indeed, all manner of cycle-specific equipment, as well as the most essential device of all – a bottle opener. It's also a wonderful 'boy toy' – the cyclist's equivalent to a Swiss army knife.

Undertaking bicycle maintenance or puncture repairs can be daunting when you don't know what you are doing. There are many cycle-maintenance classes that will teach you the basics, and the best way to learn is by doing it. A bicycle is a machine and it needs care and attention. Cyclists should check their tyres and brakes before every journey. As a bare minimum a bicycle should be serviced annually.

CARRYING LOADS

One of the joys of cycling compared to walking or hiking is that the bicycle carries your luggage. Very few cyclists carry any real weight on their backs. Those indulging in serious fitness training might be an exception but, in general, you want to cycle in comfort, especially if you are travelling a distance. That means not having anything slung over your shoulders or on your back. Panniers, made from durable waterproof materials, are hung from fitted racks on the rear and front of the bicycle. For day-to-day use, rear panniers are sufficient, but if you are touring or camping you will need more.

If you are carrying heavy loads, front panniers help to distribute weight more evenly across the bicycle and this improves your stability. Front panniers are available in two styles: standards look like regular rear panniers; low riders, which are slightly smaller, are mounted lower on the wheel for improved stability. When packing panniers try to distribute weight evenly on each side of the bicycle and remember that front panniers must carry less weight than rear panniers, as they affect steering and bike control. Also be aware that while panniers are sold as waterproof, the chances are there might be the odd leak in heavy rain. If you are visiting somewhere with a high annual rainfall and want to ensure a supply of dry clothing, waterproof pannier covers will give you the extra protection you need.

ABOVE: Let the bicycle take the strain. It's amazing what can be fitted into four panniers, a rack pack and a bar bag – enough to take you on a bicycle touring holiday.

Rack packs clip on the centre top of rear pannier frames and can also provide extra, easily accessible storage space. Ensure that the brand you buy is compatible with your pannier rack.

Bar bags hang on the handlebars and are very useful for keeping all the items you need to access regularly – wallets, cameras, maps and snacks, for example – but don't carry any real weight here. Let's not forget the old-fashioned alternative of a front basket, where you can throw all manner of handy items – the downside of such a basket is that the contents will get wet in the rain.

If you are carrying heavy loads you might want to consider a trailer – too much weight carried on a bicycle can damage it and make the bicycle unstable. Trailers can take maximum-capacity loads and make life very easy when touring. They take a little getting used to – you have to remember that you have increased length and width and make allowances when cornering. You will also have to take greater care travelling down steep hills. However, a trailer will really take the strain and allow you carry some awkward luggage that might not fit into panniers.

CYCLING WITH CHILDREN

Touring holidays by bicycle do not need to be restricted to adults only. There are plenty of options that allow you to travel with your children when they are too small to cycle themselves. Do bear in mind that they will not enjoy very long bicycle rides, so you will need to plan your route accordingly and give them lots of stops at interesting places. Seek advice on at which age to start taking your child on a bicycle seat or in a trailer; some experts advise that it is safest to wait until the child has reached one year of age.

Bicycle seats that fit onto the back of your bicycle are the classic option, but they are really only suitable for children up to the age of four or five – after that the child will be getting too heavy; it is generally recommended that you don't cycle with loads greater than 3–3½ stone (18–22kg). One of the delights of this style of child seat is that you can talk to each other as you travel. Rear child seats do affect stability, however, and learning to get your child on and off safely can take some practice.

Safety is paramount. Moulded plastic seats keep your child's feet out of the way of the wheels and give them some protection if the bicycle falls over. It is important to use over-the-shoulder, three-way safety straps – riding on a bicycle is very soporific and young children can easily fall asleep on long journeys, and can fall if not strapped in. Front child seats are really only good for short journeys as the rider is forced to adopt a bandy-legged cycling position.

Child trailers attach to the rear axle or frame of the bike and are suitable for children from the age of one to nine. They have a rigid frame and children are safely strapped in with harnesses and protected from the elements by a cover. They are still required to wear cycle helmets for added protection at all times. Trailers are low-slung, therefore they should always sport a high-visibility flag to increase motorists' awareness. As with luggage trailers, you have to get used to

WILLS'S CIGARETTES

BICYCLES ARE MADE TO CARRY ONE ONLY

LEFT: Even in 1934, cigarette cards were advocating proper seating for children, though cycle helmets and the use of bicycle seats for children is still not a legal requirement in the UK.

carrying a load behind you and to braking carefully when travelling down hills. Some trailers convert into strollers, which is useful when travelling with toddlers.

If your children want to be part of the cycling experience, but are too small to cycle independently, a trailer bicycle is an excellent solution. These fit onto the adult frame and allow children to pedal furiously, or to coast when they are worn out. It can be tiring pulling the extra weight, however, and you need to be aware of the additional width and length when cornering.

ABOVE: Established in 1924, Belstaff has been providing all-weather clothing for over 80 years. Belstaff oilskins were particularly useful for cyclists.

DON'T GET WET!

A final note on one of the most essential pieces of cycling equipment – no matter how sunny a day it is, never leave home without a waterproof. There is nothing more miserable than cycling in wet clothing. There are plenty of lightweight, waterproof jackets and ponchos to choose from. Whatever you do, make sure your waterproof is handy; I speak from experience when I say that having to empty the entire contents of your panniers to find waterproofs in a biblical downpour is not a mistake you make twice!

There is an incredible array of specialist clothing in cycle shops – you don't need them to cycle comfortably, so don't feel pressurised. If you are going any distance, however, cycle shorts can be a boon – chafing is miserable, after all, but be reassured they don't have to be in revealing skin-tight Lycra. Cyclists should layer clothing; the bottom-most layer should be close-fitting to help maintain body temperature. This method of dress allows you to strip off when hot – cycling in the rain can be hard work and a vest may be all you need under that enveloping waterproof. Cycling in winter obviously requires more in the way of specialized clothing: hats, gloves, overshoes, over-trousers and a good-quality fitted jacket are all essential.

SOUTHERN ENGLAND

*'The area of the New Forest...is probably the finest of
the large stretches of wood in England'*
Harold Briercliffe

The south of England has a soft, undulating landscape that makes for pleasant cycling. Damned with faint praise perhaps, but the south should not be underestimated. Much of the area – the most densely populated part of the country – is in London's commuter belt and is criss-crossed by motorways and railways, but you can easily escape the busy roads to explore hidden pockets of splendid countryside and mile upon mile of glorious coastline. All of it is easily accessible from London for day trips and it is studded with National Cycle Network routes.

Harold Briercliffe describes the area as 'Londoner's country' and notes that the scenery is 'pleasing rather than noble, soothing rather than inspiring'. However, for Briercliffe, what it lacks in breathtaking scenery it compensates for with 'splendid examples of ecclesiastical, military and domestic building'. He also notes that the weather is 'far kinder for the greater part of the year than it is further north'.

Cycle through the blissfully flat Kent and Essex countryside, chequered with orchards and fields of crops, and enjoy its diverse coastal landscapes of flat

BELOW: A cyclist enjoys the grass track at Hatfield Forest, where all the elements of a medieval forest survive: deer, cattle, coppice woods, pollards, scrub, timber trees, grassland and fen. **PAGE 46:** Visitors enjoying the glories of Beachy Head in 1908.

THE LONDON-TO-BRIGHTON
CYCLE RIDE

The London to Brighton run, approximately 54 miles (87 km), depending on the route, has attracted races of many descriptions over the years. It is known that a hobby-horse enthusiast challenged a coach to a race to Brighton and beat it by half an hour – although the actual date and timings are not known. In 1893 sixteen-year-old Tessie Reynolds cycled from Brighton to London and back in 8½ hours – wearing a long jacket over knickerbockers – and caused a storm of protest.

The first London to Brighton car run, the Emancipation Run, took place on 14 November 1896 – only 17 of the 33 motorists who set off arrived. The first London to Brighton Cycle Ride took place many decades later, in 1976, with around 60 participating cyclists. Only 37 finished the then 95-mile (152km) route. Today, some 27,000 cyclists take part in the annual ride, moving in vast swarms along a largely traffic-free route. The ride always takes place on a Sunday in June. Most riders take six hours to complete the course, but serious cyclists can do it in around 2½ hours. The ride is undulating and can be slow at times, but the real test for cyclists is Ditchling Beacon, close to Brighton, which climbs 700ft (213m) in just over a mile (1.6km) with a 1:4 gradient in parts.

The Naked Brighton Bike Ride started up in 2005 and is designed to illustrate the vulnerability of cyclists on the road, as well as being fun. It takes place annually, in the summer, obviously!

On the King's Road

RIGHT: The Kings Road, Brighton, in 1899 with early cyclists sharing the road with horse-riders. Despite the first cycle ride from London to Brighton at the end of the 19th century, the official London-to-Brighton bicycle race was not inaugurated until 1976.

marshland and towering cliffs. Move further west and the Sussex coast is backed by the rolling chalk hills of the South Downs, or take a boat out to the beautiful Isle of Wight to cycle England's largest offshore island. On to Hampshire and there are 49,000 acres (19,830 hectares) of heathland and woodland in the New Forest, the largest area of uncultivated land in lowland Britain. While you can't follow the course of the River Thames in its entirety, National Cycle Routes 4 and 5 take you alongside the river for stretches, then whisk you off into more scenic parts of the countryside. The Home Counties of Surrey, Berkshire, Buckinghamshire, Bedfordshire and Hertfordshire encircle London and boast some very pretty countryside and bustling market towns. To the north-west of London are the rolling chalk hills of the Chilterns, flower-strewn grassland and exquisite woodland.

Starting in Greenwich, the Garden of England Cycle Route will take you from London to Dover, along the Thames Estuary, down the south bank of the River Medway to the north Kent coast and on to Dover. The Estuary's mudflats are an essential feeding ground for important migrant bird populations and a paradise for twitchers. Dark-bellied Brent geese arrive every autumn from Siberia and, if you are lucky, you might catch a glimpse of the beautiful avocet in the summer. Follow the 18-mile (29km) Heron Trail around the Hoo Peninsula and see the maritime and rural influences of the area. Inland, the North Downs are home to rich farmland and deciduous woods filled with bluebells in the spring.

THE SOUTH COAST

The south coast of England, known as the 'gateway to England', has been at the front line in the nation's defences for centuries. It is dotted with forts, such as Richborough, castles, including the mighty Dover Castle, and fortified ports, which serve as reminders of conflicts both ancient and modern. Cycle 54 miles (87km) from Sandwich to Rye on dedicated cycle routes (National Routes 1 and 2) along quiet country lanes and coastal cliff paths. Inland, in the rolling countryside of the 'garden of England', are many stately homes and fine residences, such as Penshurst Place, Ightham Mote and Knole with cycle routes that take you right alongside. A 5-mile (8km), virtually traffic-free route runs from medieval Tonbridge Castle, one of the finest motte-and-bailey castles in England, to Penshurst Place, a medieval house with exquisite gardens.

ABOVE: A picnic on Margate beach in the 1920s. The deckchairs and golden sands are the same today, though the bathing costumes have not retained their popularity.

The 113-mile (181km) Chalk and Channel Way takes you between Dover and Folkestone, via Samphire Hoe: the newest piece of land in the country, which was created from spoil from the construction of the cross-channel tunnels. Follow the 50-mile (80km) Coast-to-Cathedral route that links Dover, Folkestone and Canterbury. Alternatively, cycle from the medieval city of Canterbury, with its magnificent cathedral, through countryside along the Crab and Winkle Way to the seaside town of Whitstable, justifiably famous for its oysters.

The area is also host to a number of charmingly faded seaside resorts, such as Margate and Broadstairs, flogging quantities of fish and chips, sticks of rock and kiss-me-quick hats evocative of seaside holidays from the 1950s and 1960s. Nature reserves, such as the salt marsh at Pegwell Bay, attract masses of birds, including the rare Sandwich tern. Explore the area along the 29-mile (46km) Viking Trail from Pegwell Bay all the way around to Reculver, near Herne Bay.

Briercliffe was rather withering about the area, but he clarifies that his dislike is limited to the 'string of crowded holiday resorts'. What was crowded in

CYCLE ROUTE

CHICHESTER *to* WEST WITTERING

WEST SUSSEX

DISTANCE: 22 MILES (35KM) RETURN TRIP   TIME: 3–4 HOURS

Salterns Way is an 11-mile (18km) cycle route from the centre of Chichester through a picturesque Chichester Harbour AONB to the sand dunes of East Head. Some of the route runs along dedicated cycle paths and other sections follow country lanes and some roads. The round trip is flat and many parts are traffic free. You should therefore allow 3 to 4 hours for the 22-mile (35km) return journey, depending on how long you stop at the various places of interest along the way.

STARTING PLACES

If you are arriving by car there are a number of pay-and-display car parks in Chichester. For those travelling by rail, the main station is just a few minutes from the starting point at the Cross.

THE ROUTE

The route starts at the Cross, Chichester **[1]**. This is where the main shopping areas of North, South, East and West Streets converge. From the Cross, travel along West Street past the Cathedral. Go straight across the roundabout into Westgate and continue **[2]**. You will need to cross the railway line before continuing into Fishbourne Road East **[3]**. Please take your time and cross carefully. An underpass brings you out on to Fishbourne Road West (A259) **[4]**. Turn left for a short way, then right on to Appledram Lane South **[5]**. After about 440 yards (400m), leave the road and go through the wooden kissing gate on your left. Sections of this route are on public footpaths, so please be courteous and give way to walkers. The path returns to Appledram Lane South through another kissing gate. Turn left at the Lane and continue to the T-junction **[6]**.

At the T-junction with Dell Quay Road turn right **[6]** and then left on to a wide farm road **[7]**. The route narrows and passes Salterns Copse woodland, then emerges at Chichester Marina **[8]**. You may want to stop here to take in the views and watch the boats entering and leaving the marina. Turn left and travel around the marina. Shortly after the car barrier, turn right **[9]** and keep on the road alongside Chichester Canal until you reach the second bridge crossing the canal adjacent to the old lock gates **[10]**. This is a public footpath; you must dismount and walk over the bridge. Turn right at the end of the tall fence, then continue to the road.

Stay on Lock Lane, which becomes Broomers Lane then Martins Lane. You will come to a junction with Church Lane. Turn right **[11]** and continue along Church Lane, passing the church on your left. Church Lane then becomes Westlands Lane, which is a concrete road leading down to a farm. Just before the farm you will see two gates to your left. Go through the small kissing gate **[12]** and follow the route that crosses fields before coming out next to Itchenor Caravan Park.

After passing the caravan park go through the wooden gate and turn right on to Itchenor Road **[13]**. Follow the road round to the right. Pass the church of St Nicholas on your right; 50 yards on, turn left **[14]**. Do not continue down the road to Itchenor Park Farm but take the left turn that goes to the village hall and pass through the small wooden gate. Follow the signed path until you come to a junction with a concrete farm road. Turn left on this road and continue until you see the path on the right. The cycle route continues across the field; a gate at the other end takes you through to Sheepwash Lane. Turn right on to Sheepwash Lane **[15]**. This lane is used by vehicles and horses; please cycle with care. Continue until you come to Rookwood Road **[16]**.

Turn right on to Rookwood Road **[16]**. This is a busier road, please cycle with care and watch out for traffic. You will pass a small row of shops; continue on and turn right into Pound Road. Pass the public toilets on your left and bear left on to the road that takes you down to the West Wittering beach car park **[17]**. This road can be very busy on summer weekends with traffic queuing to get into the car park. Follow the road right down to the car-park entrance. Cycle through the car park to the far end. At the end proceed on foot through the five-bar gate and on to East Head **[18]**. You may want to take a break here; there are many wonderful birds to be seen and you can enjoy the wide open sands and views of the South Downs and Chichester Harbour. Alternatively, stop off in nearby West Wittering village before retracing your route back to Chichester.

Briercliffe's day is likely to be struggling to attract tourists today. The south coast is much changed for cyclists and there are now some excellent cycle routes covering the area that keep you well away from busy main roads.

THE SOUTH DOWNS

Moving westwards around the coast you come to the South Downs, an area of chalk downland with rolling hills and valleys covering some 530 square miles (1,374 sq km). It stretches across the south-east of England, running along the sea coast of East Sussex from Beachy Head to Brighton and Hove, then up through West Sussex and over to Winchester on the eastern side of Hampshire. Two areas within the Downs are designated Areas of Outstanding Natural Beauty: East Hampshire AONB and Sussex Downs AONB. They contain 670 scheduled ancient monuments, the undulating Seven Sisters cliffs and Devil's Dyke Valley, the largest dry valley in the UK.

Cross the South Downs via the 100-mile (160km) national trail, The South Downs Way, and the southern portion of the Monarch's Way. It is a stunning ride, but chunks of it are cross-country and only suitable for off-road mountain bikes. Large areas of the South Downs are mixed woodland but at Kingley Vale Nature Reserve, close to the Cycle Chichester Sustrans route, is one of the finest yew forests in Western Europe, containing gnarled trees more than 2,000 years old. Tackle a run down to Brighton and enjoy the extravaganza of the Royal Pavilion or take the off-road Cheesefoot Head cycle route to Winchester, the capital of England in Saxon and Norman times. Winchester cathedral, built in the Norman era, is one of the longest cathedrals in Europe.

ABOVE: Cyclists coasting down Newtimber Hill on the Devil's Dyke Estate can see some of the best chalk grassland in the country.

THE ISLE OF WIGHT

Sitting in the Solent, opposite Portsmouth, is The Isle of Wight. The island offers much more than a pretty holiday location for it contains a remarkable diversity of landscapes: wooded valleys, chalk grasslands, all manner of coastline and cliffscapes and the marshy basin of the River Yar. According to Harold Briercliffe: 'The tourist who wishes to choose a small, neat region for exploration from a single centre could hardly better, in southern England, the delightful Isle of Wight,' though he cautions 'wheelmen' against travelling in July and August when the roads are likely to be busy. There are many designated cycle routes around the island, some off-road, but many country lanes are quiet and pleasant to cycle (see also pages 61–67).

ABOVE: Professor Edward J. Reddish performs his 'Celebrated Bicycle Dive' off the pier at Worthing in 1902.

THE NEW FOREST

The New Forest is the largest area of uncultivated land in the south – 36,000 acres (14,569 hectares) of broadleaved pasture woodland where mature trees are under-grazed. Harold Briercliffe described it as, 'A great natural heritage, in many respects a survival of the England of the days before the Norman conquest.' Oak and beech dominate the most mature woodland, but birch, hawthorn, ash, Scots pine, holly and sweet chestnut can be seen along with unusual species, such as wellingtonia.

Much more than just an ancient woodland landscape, the New Forest contains tracts of heath, grassland and valley bogs and is home to an outstanding array of wildlife; red, fallow and roe deer, badgers, 13 species of bat and the famous New Forest ponies. One hundred and fifty scheduled ancient monuments and 250 round-barrow burial grounds bear testament to the lives of early Stone Age and Bronze Age settlers. William the Conqueror made it a Royal Forest in 1079, recorded as *Nova Foresta* in the Domesday Book in 1086. Deer and wild pig were protected for the exclusive pleasure of the monarch. The New Forest Cycle Network links New Forest villages via gravel tracks and quiet country roads and there are more than 100 miles (160km) of traffic-free routes running through it.

NEOLITHIC COUNTRYSIDE

North of the New Forest, on Salisbury Plain in Wiltshire, is the World Heritage Site of Stonehenge, consisting of earthworks enclosing large standing stones. The stone circle is estimated to date from between 3000–1600 BC and originally featured 80 stones, some of which were transported from Wales. It is unique in that it is the only stone circle to have lintels around the top. Avebury, just

BELOW: A tandem glides past Stonehenge in the 1930s. Cyclists, walkers and drivers could still run directly past this incredible World Heritage Site.

2 miles (3.2km) east of Stonehenge, is also a designated World Heritage Site and home to one of Europe's largest stone circles. It is a Neolithic monument estimated to be around 5000 years old. A giant monolith stands in the centre, and avenues of stones lead in and out of the circle. Many of the original stones were destroyed, though some were re-erected in the 1930s. Unlike at Stonehenge, it is still possible to walk freely around the area. The 16-mile (26km) Woodford Valley Circuit takes you past the River Avon and on to the archaeology of the great earthwork of Old Sarum, near Salisbury, and Stonehenge.

Follow the River Avon on the 28-mile (45km) Avon Valley Explorer, which runs from Pewsey through the Vale of The White Horse, via Stonehenge and Old Sarum Castle to Salisbury Cathedral. There are 13 chalk figures to be seen in Wiltshire, both animal and human forms. Some are estimated to be 3,000 years old, but most are a mere 300 years old. Take the Salisbury Plain Explorer and cycle the range from Westbury White Horse to Pewsey Vale. The western section of the Ridgeway Trail runs from Avebury up to Streatley on the River Thames, and some stretches east of the river into the Chilterns.

THE CHILTERNS

Moving up into the Home Counties, the Chilterns, in north Berkshire and Buckinghamshire, are a designated Area of Outstanding Natural Beauty. They cover some 322 square miles (833 sq km). The Hills lie north-west of London and stretch from the Thames Valley in Oxfordshire on a 47-mile (75km) diagonal, north-east trajectory through Buckingham and Bedfordshire and on up to Hitchin in Hertfordshire. The boundary is clearly defined on the north-west side by the scarp slope. It subsides to the south-east and naturally dips through sloping countryside, merging with the landscape. Famous for undulating chalk hills containing some of the most beautiful tracts of beech woodland in the country, the area is spectacular in spring – hazy with bluebells – and glowing with warm colours in autumn. It offers a range of cycling options to suit both families and off-roaders. The highest point in the Chilterns is Haddington Hill in Wendover Woods in Buckinghamshire which reaches 876ft (267m). Ivinghoe Beacon, home to a Bronze Age Hill Fort, comes a close second at 817ft (249m). It marks the start of the Icknield Way, one of the oldest roads in the UK and in existence even before the Romans came to Britain. It is reserved exclusively for walkers, but the Icknield Way Trail, which is currently

CYCLE ROUTE

OLD WARDEN
Circular Route
BEDFORDSHIRE

DISTANCE: 16½ MILES (26.5KM)   TIME: APPROX 2 HOURS

This circular route passes through a series of villages nestling in the English countryside. The 16½ mile (26.5 km) route should take around 2 hours to cycle, or longer if you stop at places along the way, such as the Shuttleworth Collection.

STARTING PLACES

A good place to start for those arriving by car is the car park next to St Leonard's Church in Old Warden. If you want to arrive by train you will need to cycle from Bedford and start the route at Cardington. Details of a suitable cycle link from Bedford can be found on the Bedfordshire County Council website. It is suggested that you follow an anti-clockwise direction.

Map labels:

to Cambridge
A421
to Bedford
A603
to Willington
to Milton Keynes
to Harrowden
5 Cople
6 Cardington
Mox Hill
College Wood
disused railway
0   1 mile
0   1 km
Manor Farm
Home Wood
4 Northill
Hillfoot Farm
Ickwell
St Leonard's Church
2
3 to Biggleswade
BEDFORD ROAD
1 †
Shuttleworth Collection
Old Warden
7   **13**
SCHOOL LANE
8
12 Southill
9
10   **11**

THE ROUTE

If starting from the car park next to St Leonard's Church you should cycle down the lane to the main road and turn left **[1]**. Follow the road from Old Warden towards Ickwell. You should take the first left turn for Ickwell **[2]** but may want to stop near this point to visit the famous Shuttleworth Collection, an aeronautical and automotive museum located at the Old Warden airfield. It hosts a huge variety of old but well-preserved aircraft.

Continuing left at the junction you are soon in Ickwell. When you reach the centre of the village continue straight on at the T-junction, following the sign for Northill [3]. At Northill, take the first turn to the left, which is signed for Cople [4]. This part of the route takes you past Home Wood on your left and College Wood on your right. The road gradually climbs up towards Mox

ABOVE: Shuttleworth College from Old Warden, Bedfordshire.

Hill then starts to fall again as you head towards Cople. When you arrive in the village you should take the left turn for Cardington [5]. As you cycle through Cardington you should ignore the right turn for Harrowden and instead follow the road around to the left and on towards Southill [6].

The next section of the route runs parallel to a dismantled railway and goes past Manor Farm and Hillfoot Farm. You should continue straight on along Bedford Road until you reach the T-junction with Old Warden (a left here would provide an early return to your starting point at St Leonard's Church) [7]. To enjoy the full route you should turn right at this junction and continue to cycle south along the hedge-lined lane until you pass under the old railway bridge. At this point you should turn left following the sign for Southill [8]. This is a wonderful lane through woodland that has a dense canopy during the summer months. As you come out of the wooded area you will need to turn left [9], then left again [10]. You will reach another side road, where you should turn left once more and head towards Southill [11]. As you enter Southill you should follow the bend in the road around to the right, then turn left back along School Lane towards Old Warden [12]. You will cycle past a lake on your left and through woods before arriving at a T-junction with Bedford Road [13]. Turn right here and make your way back to the start point at St Leonard's Church.

under development, runs roughly parallel to the walker's route and can be used by both cyclists and horse riders.

The Severn and Thames Cycle Route runs through much of the Home Counties on its 128-mile (206km) route, around half of which is traffic-free. It starts on the borders with Wales by the Severn, moves over to the Avon Valley, goes over the Wiltshire Downs into the Thames Valley at Newbury and continues on to Reading.

The county of Bedfordshire has undulating chalk hills and quiet, pretty villages, especially in the north of the county. The River Ouse winds its way through and many tributaries join it. Don't miss the magnificent stately home Woburn Abbey. John Bunyan spent much of his life in this county and you can see where he lived at Elstow. A section of the University Way cycle route runs through Bedfordshire between Sandy and Milton Keynes via the centre of Bedford and is a pretty, traffic-free route.

ABOVE: A group of cyclists preparing for a race in Walsworth, Hertfordshire, taken on 13 August 1939, just three weeks before the outbreak of the Second World War. The picture was taken by Harold Briercliffe.

CLARE'S ISLE OF WIGHT JOURNEY
ANOTHER LAND

'Throughout this journey I've heard stories of escapism – stories of people who have come to the Isle of Wight to unshackle themselves from the everyday world. Everyone from Darwin to Dickens and Queen Victoria to Karl Marx! This place represents the ultimate in escapism and fantasy, as it is the home of the real life Alice in Wonderland – Alice Liddell. It really is quite extraordinary, the list of people who have come here and been inspired.'

CLARE BALDING

Harold Briercliffe describes the Isle of Wight as 'another land, distinct, fascinating and, on acquaintance, lovable'. Like any number of illustrious characters before him, including Charles Darwin, Charles Dickens and Alfred, Lord Tennyson, he loved the Island's sense of escapism, of otherness and its separation from familiar Britain.

The Isle of Wight has an extremely varied landscape. As Briercliffe observes, 'the rhomboid off the south coast is a geological mix-up and that fact in itself ensures its variety'. More than half of the island is a designated Area of Outstanding Natural Beauty.

Our journey starts in an old underground train that runs overground from Ryde to Shanklin, the start of a cycling odyssey in Shanklin. Interestingly, even in Briercliffe's day the transport system was quaint – he describes it as 'a delightful relic from another day'. Looking at the old and new parts of the town the changes from Harold Briercliffe's day are all too easy

ABOVE: Clare Balding en route to Winterbourne, where Charles Dickens lived for a while and wrote part of *Great Expectations*.

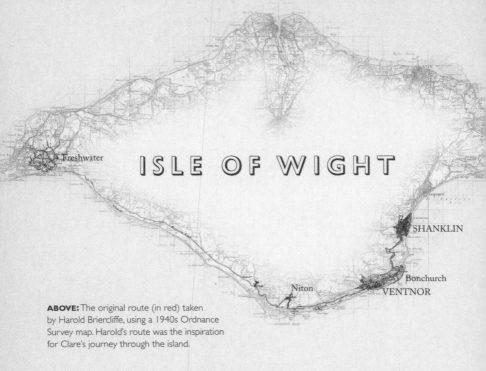

ISLE OF WIGHT

Freshwater

SHANKLIN

Niton

Bonchurch
VENTNOR

ABOVE: The original route (in red) taken
by Harold Briercliffe, using a 1940s Ordnance
Survey map. Harold's route was the inspiration
for Clare's journey through the island.

to spot – notably the pier, which he describes as all too easy to miss but which is
now entirely invisible, as it was demolished in the 1980s.

INSPIRING DARWIN

Another notable visitor was Charles Darwin, who moved his family to the
Island from their home in Shropshire to escape the scarlet-fever epidemic.
He wrote of Shanklin that it was the nicest seaside place he had ever seen. He
stayed at Norfolk House in the 1850s and began writing *On the Origin of Species*.
Norfolk House is now the Waterfront Inn and visitors can take a drink, have
a meal, or even stay in what was Darwin's home. It is incredible to think that
Darwin found the inspiration right here to begin writing his masterpiece. For
18 months he wrote in Shanklin the 'different view' of mankind's history, which
would revolutionize our understanding of who we are and where we came from.
What was it about the Isle of Wight that inspired him?

SHANKLIN CHINE

Don't leave the area without visiting Shanklin Chine, a ravine formed over the past 10,000 years, which drops from 105ft (32m) to sea level. At the top of the ravine near the village is a 45ft (14m) waterfall. The Chine then runs for just over ¾ mile (1km) down to the esplanade. This natural feature has a colourful past; it was used by smugglers and invaders across the centuries and in the Second World War was the start of a 65-mile (105km) pipeline, known as PLUTO (Pipeline Under the Ocean) that ran under the English Channel to Cherbourg, supplying troops with 56,000 gallons (255,000 litres) of fuel a day.

Shanklin Chine became a tourist spot in the eighteenth century. Jane Austen and John Keats both commented on the feature and it was a major Victorian tourist attraction, pulling in such luminaries as Charles Dickens, George Eliot and Henry W. Longfellow. In 1873 the entrance fee was six old pennies (2½ new pence); the price stuck until 1958.

RIGHT: A romantic illustration of the steep-sided Shanklin Chine from 1908. Today, in summer, the Chine is transformed at night by illuminations, a facility not on offer a hundred years ago.

CHARLES DICKENS' *DAVID COPPERFIELD*

South of Shanklin is the village of Bonchurch, where you can find the church that Harold Briercliffe describes as 'small and plain, but beautified outside by roses and creepers'. The village is named after St Boniface, who preached to the island's fishermen from what is known as Pulpit Rock. Close to the church is Winterbourne, once home to Charles Dickens, now a B&B. The story goes that he had completed four chapters of *David Copperfield*, but the fifth was giving him some trouble, so he left London for a breath of sea air. He fell in love with the island, describing it as the prettiest place he had seen in the world, and found the inspiration to complete that elusive chapter in what is now known as the Copperfield Room. Swinburne and Keats also stayed in the village.

Inland between Bonchurch and Ventnor is St Boniface Down. At around 800ft (243m) it is the highest point of the island. Bronze Age burial grounds bear witness to the longevity of the island. Charles Dickens walked here from Bonchurch daily during his stay. Harold Briercliffe was not quite so inspired by the landscape – he saw this place more as a blot, disfigured by its radar station. Built at the start of the Second World War as part of the Chain Home radar system set up to defend the British coastline from the air, the station played a key role in the tracking and interception of enemy bombers. Today it is home to mobile-phone and communication masts linking the island to the wider world.

Briercliffe's mood lifts on the descent towards Cook's Castle, a viewpoint 562ft (171m) above sea level: 'All of the northern half of the island can be seen from the Freshwater Cliffs in the west, to Culver Cliff in the east. Below lies Wroxall in its vee-valley – across which appears the Worsley Monument at the

BELOW: Clare Balding pedals into Bonchurch during her Isle of Wight tour. Dickens, Swinburne and Keats were earlier visitors.

end of a parallel ridge, also pointing northward. To the right of this can be seen Godshill Church and, again to the right, Carisbrook Castle.' A castle has sat on this site since Saxon times, though the existing castle was started in 1100 and extensively rebuilt in 1262. Charles I was imprisoned here between 1647 and 1648; he tried to escape but got wedged in the window bars.

THE GRADIENTS OF VENTNOR

Dropping from Boniface Down to Ventnor requires care: 'Because of the precipitousness of its site, Ventnor is laid out in terraces and along these, going from west to east, or in reverse, the gradients are very slight indeed. Dropping down to the pier, however, from the station, is quite an adventure. The gradients at the hairpins between one terrace and the one above or below are as steeps as the turns are sharp and the utmost caution must be observed.'

Harold Briercliffe described the resort as once being exclusive, perhaps suggesting that pre-war the town was somewhat snobbish. By the 1940s he described it as 'a go-ahead place, with plenty of accommodation, shops and cinemas'. He was sad to note that the pier, broken as an invasion precaution, had not been restored to its pre-war glory. He would doubtless have been pleased that it was rebuilt in 1955, but distressed to learn that it fell into disrepair after a fire in 1985 and was finally demolished in 1993.

RIGHT: An advertisement from 1922 for the Royal Court Hotel in Ventnor promises visitors sunshine and comfort.

UNDERCLIFF

Out of Ventnor, the Undercliff runs along the southern edge of the island. It was formed when the upper strata of chalk slipped over a band of softer clay, creating a tumbling landscape full of lush green vegetation. Briercliffe described it as 'one of the most impressive natural features of the island and regarded as the most picturesque stretch of country on it'. The microclimate here was recognized as being beneficial to health, an additional draw for the sickly Victorians. Karl Marx was sent to the island by his doctor three times and a young Winston Churchill came here to convalesce.

Take a small detour off the main route down to the villages of Niton Undercliff and Niton, which Briercliffe describes as commanding a 'remarkable panorama of the uniform south-west coast as far as The Needles'. Out at sea, look for St Catherine's Lighthouse, known locally as the Pepperpot, which was bombed in a direct hit in the Second World War, killing three lighthouse keepers. Nearby is the Buddle Inn, a sixteenth-century hostelry reputed to be a haunt of smugglers in bygone days. Harold Briercliffe endearingly describes it as 'a sophisticated roadhouse'.

Our journey followed Harold Briercliffe's route along the spectacular Military Road, which runs off the south-west coast of the island. Today, however, it is very busy with traffic, and not ideal for cycling. Due to its position the Island has always been the first line of defence for Britain's south coast. It has been under attack for centuries, though the current adversary is the wind, which is eroding the fragile cliffs.

At the western end of Military Road, high on chalk cliffs above the village of Freshwater, is Tennyson Down, named after the Victorian poet who sought tranquility and inspiration here. Tennyson walked on the downs where the chalk-white cliffs reach their highest point, 482 feet (147m) above sea level, marked with the Tennyson Memorial. The downs continue west, ending at the Needles. The Needles – three chalk stacks that rise out of the sea beyond the western tip of the island – take their name from the shape of a fourth pillar, which was known as Lot's Wife and was actually needle-shaped, which collapsed in a storm in 1764. Cyclists can enjoy the off-road Tennyson Trail, which boasts incredible views of this section of the island and its distinctive landmarks.

ALFRED, LORD TENNYSON

Tennyson and his wife Emily moved to Farringford in Freshwater shortly after he was appointed Poet Laureate in 1850, and they lived there for 40 years. Freshwater inspired him to write some of his greatest poetry, including 'Maud' and 'Idylls of the King' as well as the great elegy 'Crossing the Bar', which follows the journey from the mainland across the Solent. The house, now a hotel, attracted visiting intelligentsia, including Charles Darwin, the first female photographer Julia Margaret Cameron and the Italian revolutionary Garibaldi. Dimbola Lodge in Freshwater Bay was Cameron's studio and is now a museum housing much of her extraordinary work.

'Sunset and evening star,
And one clear call for me!
And may there be no moaning of the bar,
When I put out to sea,
But such a tide as moving seems asleep,
Too full for sound and foam,
When that which drew from out the
*   boundless deep*
Turns again home'
Alfred, Lord Tennyson 'Crossing the Bar'

Our journey ends here and highlights Harold Briercliffe's view that there is plenty to see on the island. He also notes that 'the influence of the sea and a reputation for mildness and sunniness makes the Isle of Wight a favourite out-of-season touring ground for cyclists.' The favourable climate provides the icing on the cake — the Isle of Wight is a perfect place to tour by bicycle.

ABOVE: A Julia Margaret Cameron photograph of the steep slip at Freshwater Bay, geographically part of the chalk hills that stretch from Devon to Dover.

BRISTOL CHANNEL

SOMERSET

Linton
Countesbury
Martinhoe
Brendon
Combe Martin
Paracombe
Ilfracombe
Mortehoe
Kentisbury
Berry Narbor
Trentishoe

Morte Bay
W. Down
Arlington
Challacombe
Loxhore
Stoke Rivers
High Bray
Charles
N. Molton
Buckland
Twitchen
Molland

Barnstaple
Braunton
Heanton Punchardon
Ashford
Pilton
Goodleigh
Swim bridge
Bishop's Tawton
Fremington
Bickington

Barnstaple Bay
Appledore
Northam
Bideford
Abbotsham
Littleham
Wear Gifford
Monkleigh
Brewers
Frithelstock
Buckland Brewer

Dulverton
Morebath
Bampton
Huntsham
Hockworthy

Landcross
Huish
Yarnscombe
Atherington
High Bickington
Chulmleigh
Chawleigh
Cheldon
Witheridge
Templeton
Tiverton
Calverleigh
Washfield
Stoodleigh

Putford
Bulkworthy
Newton Petrock
Shebbear
Sheepwash
Peters Marland
Merton
Dolton
Dowland
Monks Brushford
Zeal Monachorum
Morchard
Cadeleigh
Bickleigh
Silverton
Colebrooke
Crediton
Shobrook
Collumpton
Bradninch

Holsworthy
Hollacombe
Pyworthy
Clawton
Halwill
Ashwater
Germans Week
Bradworthy
Virginstow
Broadwood Widger
Stowford
Lew Trenchard
Lifton
Mary Stow
Bridestow
Sourton
Throwley
Gidleigh
Chagford
Moreton Hampstead
North Bovey
Manaton
Lustleigh

Hatherleigh
Jacobstow
Inwardleigh
Exbourne
Sampford Courtenay
Honey Church
Bow
Bow Church
Colebrooke
Newton
Cheriton Bishop
Whitestone
Tedburn
Dunsford
Holcombe Burnell
St Thomas
EXETER
Topsham
Powderham
Kenton
Mamhead
Dawlish
Teignmouth

Okehampton
Tawton
Throwleigh
Dartmoor Forest
Mary Tavy
Peter Tavy
Brentor
Lamerton
Milton Abbots
Sydenham Damerel
Tavistock
Whitchurch
Sampford Spiney
Widecombe in the Moor
Buckland in the Moor
Ashburton
Teigngrace
Newton Bushel
Kingsteignton
Bishopsteignton
Chudleigh
Ashcombe

Beer Alston
Beer Ferrers
Tamerton Foliot
Buckland Monachorum
Sheepstor
Walkhampton
Meavy
Sheepstor
Holne
Buckfastleigh
Dean Church
Staverton
Rattery
Dean Prior

Saltash
Stoke Damerel
St Budeaux
Plympton Earle
Brixton
Plymstock
Devonport
Plymouth
Holbeton
Yealmpton
Brixton
Modbury
Ermington
Ugborough
Diptford
Harberton
Ashprington
Cornwood
Harford

Totnes
Berry Head
Brixham
Kingswear
Torbay
Tor Quay
St Mary Church
Coffinswell
Kingskerswell

Plymouth Sound
Rame Head
Newton Ferrers
Revelstoke
Wembury
Kingston
Aveton Giffard
Bigbury
Thurlestone
Modbury
Woodleigh
Blackawton
Dartmouth
Stoke Fleming
Kingsbridge
Stokenham
Start Bay
Slapton
Start Point
Chivelstone

Stoke Gabriel
Dittisham
Halwell
Charleton
Churchstow

SOUTH-WEST ENGLAND

'The coastline is incomparably the finest and the grandest in the country' Harold Briercliffe

The South-West boasts a warm climate, mile upon mile of breathtaking coastline, beautiful beaches and a wealth of landscapes from rich farmland to forests and moorland – its attractions have been evident to man since prehistoric times. The area is home to an abundance of cycle routes to suit all tastes from the relative novice to families and serious off-road tourers. At the tip of the foot of England is Cornwall, a Celtic stronghold with sections of sub-tropical coastline. It is separated from Devon by the River Tamar, which flows along all but 5 miles (8km) of the border, making it a virtual island; wherever you are in the county, the sea is never further than 20 miles (32km) away. Devon is dominated by the granite uplands of Dartmoor; the north coast has pretty beaches and a bracing aspect, while the south coast is warmer with palm trees and sub-tropical flowers. There is rich farmland in Somerset, while the limestone Mendip Hills contain spectacular caves and gorges. The fine cities of Bristol and Bath sit at the northernmost tip of the area. Dorset is a rural county with many spectacular seaside towns, including Lyme Regis, Weymouth and Swanage. The Jurassic Coast, which runs along the southern coastline of Dorset and Devon, is a geological paradise with rocks that showcase 185 million years of evolution.

BELOW: A mountain biker rides cross-country near the Bristol Channel. Briercliffe recommends a four-day tour of the area, starting at Taunton and stopping at Wells, Weston-super-Mare and Bath, 'the most beautiful city in England'. **PAGE 88:** A map of Devon c. 1857.

Harold Briercliffe was a little waspish on the subject of the South-West: 'Let it be admitted at the beginning that much of the coast of Devon and Cornwall in high summer provides little or no solitude for the wanderer awheel. Villages that the old guidebook writers found to be quaint or picturesque have now been "improved" out of all recognition. Coves which were remote and unfrequented 50 years ago have become as sophisticated as a cinema foyer. The road between Penzance and Land's End has as many buses and cars as Piccadilly… A multitude does not itself prevent the appreciation of fine scenery, but a litter of bungalows, huts and concrete in its midst can cause revulsion to rise in the breast of the man who has cycled 500 miles to find peace.'

As he observes, the South-West hardly boasts the open wilderness of mid-Wales, Northumberland or the Scottish Highlands; its attractions are altogether different but no less alluring. The advent of fast motorways and A-roads has removed many vehicles from the old, meandering routes and the profusion of cycle routes makes the area very enticing. Briercliffe warms to the region, describing it as '… a huge playground, stabilized and made friendly by an ever-present background of husbandry and all that is best in English country life. Therein lies its appeal to the touring cyclist from the towns and therein lies the reason for the South-West being the most popular holiday district in Britain for the organised wheelman.'

BRISTOL AND SOMERSET

The historic trading port of Bristol, home to the National Cycle Network Centre, has some excellent cycle routes, though parts of the city are very hilly. Follow the Bristol-to-Bath railway path and explore the best-preserved Georgian city in Britain with its hot springs and Roman baths. The notoriously hard-to-please Briercliffe observed: 'Bath can be said to be the most beautiful city in England.' Follow the West Country Way from Bristol or Bath all the way down to Padstow in Cornwall – a journey of 240 miles (386km), 70 (113km) of which are traffic-free. Serious touring cyclists will enjoy the challenge of the Mendip Hills, not least the fast descent into the 7-mile (11km) long Cheddar Gorge and the weary, slow ascent out the other side. Impressive caves can be seen at Cheddar and Wookey.

Further south you will find the Quantock Hills, which cover an area of just 38 square miles (99 sq km): a little less demanding, especially the hills on the eastern side, which drop down to the plains. The area is renowned for its

beauty and inspired the poets Coleridge and Wordsworth. The crest of the Quantocks gives views north across to where the Severn Estuary meets the sea, east over to the Mendips, south down to the heartlands of Somerset and west to Exmoor. Between the Quantocks and the Mendips lie the Somerset Levels, a sparsely populated wetland plain. Willows grow here in abundance and have long been used for baskets and fencing; the fertile grassland provided materials for thatching. Tors, such as Glastonbury, which Briercliffe describes as resembling the pyramids, and Barrow Mump stand out on the horizon. It is a breeding ground for many bird species, including the Bewicks swan, snipe and the marsh harrier. The area is wonderfully flat and ideal for cycling, with many designated routes.

DEVON AND CORNWALL

The Exmoor National Park takes the cyclist through contrasting changes of scenery from Somerset into Devon. It covers 267 square miles (692 sq km) and is primarily moorland, though 34 miles (55km) of the area is coastline with imposing cliffs and the craggy terrain of the Brendon Hills, cut through by streams and rivers. There is evidence of occupation since Mesolithic times and Exmoor contains 208 scheduled ancient monuments. The National Park encompasses the longest stretch of coastal woodland in the country, the Exmoor Forest, described by Briercliffe as 'the crowning glory of the Atlantic Coast'.

The Exmoor Cycle Route is a 60-mile (96km) circular trail; Minehead is the recommended start and finish point because of its public transport links. It runs to Porlock, onto Lynton and Lynmouth, across the countryside to Wheddon Cross and Elworthy before doubling back to Minehead and can be tackled in a day or broken into touring sections. Alternatively, follow the north Devon coast beyond Exmoor from Trentishoe to Welcombe and you will find dramatic coastal scenery with towering cliffs and the tourist resorts of Ilfracombe, Appledore and Clovelly. Harold Briercliffe liked Clovelly in spite of himself: 'Trippers and four-legged donkeys jostle each other all summer down its steep, stepped, "main street". Yet despite all this popularity, the beauty and charm of Clovelly are indisputable.'

Dartmoor, the largest area of open country in the south of England, covers an area just short of 368 square miles (1,000 sq km). It is wetter, warmer and windier than much of the UK; the prevailing wind comes from the south-west or west and is laden with moisture from the mid-Atlantic drift – hence the local saying: 'Nine months winter and three months bad weather.' It was established as a National Park in 1951 and contains a rich diversity of wildlife

ABOVE: The donkeys at Clovelly, seen here in 1908, were used to cart essentials from the harbour up the steep cobbled streets of the village. The practice only ceased in the 1990s, but donkeys are still seen here today.

CYCLE ROUTE

COAST to COAST
on the MINERAL TRAMWAY
CORNWALL

DISTANCE: 22 MILES (35KM) RETURN TRIP   TIME: 3½ HOURS

The Mineral Tramways Trail provides a unique and fascinating 11-mile (17km) cycle route from Portreath to Devoran, crossing the West Cornwall Peninsula. The route follows what were once busy working rail and tram tracks that carried coal, tin and copper to bustling quays at Devoran and Portreath. Portreath was once a busy port importing coal and exporting copper, but it is now a pretty resort, popular with surfers. Devoran, your destination, has a similar past, exporting copper and importing timber, coal and iron, but it developed as a 'new town' in the nineteenth century.

The redundant tram and rail tracks have gradually been brought back into use as cycling and walking routes. The combination of old tracks with a few quiet country lanes now provides an excellent quiet and generally flat link from the Atlantic to the south Cornish coast.

It will take around 3½ hours to cycle the 22-mile (35km) round trip. If you want to stop and appreciate the many places of interest along the way you will need to allow much more time, maybe even a whole day.

STARTING PLACES

There are two suggested starting places on the north coast but you may just as easily choose to start on the south coast at Devoran. The first is at Portreath. If arriving by car you can park in the public car park near the beach. This gets very busy during the summer months and you may need to look for another parking place within the town. Alternatively, you may find it much easier to park at the nearby Elm Farm Cycle Centre at Cambrose. This is just 2 miles (3km) along the cycle trail from Portreath and offers free car parking as well as cycle hire and other facilities, including bicycle maintenance.

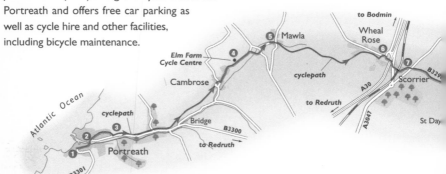

THE ROUTE

Starting at the public car park in Portreath **[1]**, you will need to turn left along Tregea Terrace. When you reach the junction next to the Portreath Arms Hotel you cycle in to Sunnyvale Road **[2]**, then join the cycle path that runs alongside the B3300 out of the town **[3]**. Keep following the cycle path and you will reach Cambrose. Here you will find the alternative starting location at Elm Farm Cycle Centre **[4]**. This is a great place to start if you want to hire a bike or wish to avoid the crowds and traffic of Portreath during the peak summer months.

Follow the signs guiding you out of Cambrose along the quiet country lanes that lead to Mawla. At this point **[5]** you rejoin the cycle path once again. The path continues to rise gradually as you head towards Wheal Rose **[6]**. At this point you come off the path and join a short section of the A3047, which takes you over the A30 (take care) and into Scorrier **[7]**. Here you rejoin the cycle path again as it takes you out of Scorrier and gradually downhill into the Poldice Valley, then alongside the Carnon River. This part of the route takes you through a landscape that still reflects the mining activity that was so extensive in the past; mine shafts and mine buildings are still visible.

Eventually you will reach a crossing at the busy A39 where you need to take special care **[8]**, after which you arrive in Devoran **[9]**. You may want to retrace your journey at this point and cycle back along the 11-mile (17km) route towards Portreath.

Alternatively, you may want to explore the picturesque estuary by cycling on along the minor roads towards Feock. Here you can take a ferry over to Falmouth and visit the town and Pendennis Castle, which marks the end of a chain of defensive structures built by Henry VIII.

Further information about this route and the facilities available at Elm Farm Cycle Centre can be found at www.cornwallcycletrails.com.

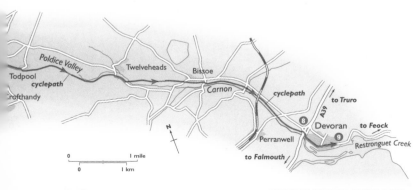

ABOVE: The Camel Trail is possibly one of the most popular cycle routes in the country, running for some 17 traffic-free miles (27km) through exquisite countryside to the Cornish coast.

and flora as well as more than 1,000 scheduled ancient monuments and 2,500 listed buildings. Around 65 per cent of Dartmoor is made up of 280 million-year-old rock. The granite core of Dartmoor is surrounded by sedimentary rocks, such as limestone, sandstone and shale. There are more than 160 granite tors on Dartmoor; the height of the tors and the exposed landscape often produce extremes of weather.

Cornwall offers a huge array of landscapes, from the tumbling tourist-trap tip of Land's End, where only five miles (8km) of land divides the raging Atlantic from the English Channel, to picturesque fishing villages, bleak moorland, the tumbling Atlantic surf of Newquay and the gentle beaches of the Cornish Riviera. The Cornish Way details 180 miles (289km) of named cycle routes in the county. Trails run from Bude down to Bodmin Moor and out to Tintagel Castle, famously associated with Arthurian legend. Bodmin is a compact moor of around 80 square miles (208 sq km); great granite tors stand out, the best known of which is Brown Willy, the highest point in Cornwall. The Camel Trail is possibly one of the most ridden cycle trails in the whole of the UK; it runs for some 17 miles (27km) from Padstow through Wadebridge to Bodmin on a disused rail track. You can trek right down to Land's End on The First and Last Trail which takes you from Phillack, close to St Ives on the north coast, cross-country to Penzance on the south coast where you have stunning views of St Michael's Mount. The last leg takes you out to Land's End via Mousehole, the quintessential narrow Cornish village, and St Buryan, known for its 12 standing stones.

The Lizard Peninsula, the most southerly point in the UK, has some of the most beautiful scenery in the country. This rugged outcrop of rock, with sea on two sides and the Helford River to the north, has an extraordinarily mild climate, which has led to the growth of some sub-tropical vegetation. The coast from the Lizard all around the Cornish Riviera from Helford to Mevagissey is dotted with tiny fishing villages tucked into small coves that are accessible by narrow roads sunk between banks of wild flowers, all blessed with a blissfully mild climate. The country lanes are quiet outside the school holidays and make interesting touring.

The South Hams, the most southerly part of Devon, has the mildest climate in Britain – some flowers still bloom in December. It runs from Totnes to Prawle Point north to south and extends from Plymouth to Dartmouth west to east. This hilly, agricultural area is subdivided by rivers; there are cycle routes, some of which utilize ferry crossings, so it is useful to check ferry times before you travel. Similarly hilly is the rural heartland of Devon situated between Dartmoor and Exmoor; it's less popular with tourists, the roads can be tranquil out of season and there are many good cycle routes to explore.

ABOVE: Kynance Cove, on the Lizard Peninsula, has long been considered one of the most beautiful places in Cornwall. Briercliffe recommended a minimum stay of two nights to explore the area fully.

THE JURASSIC COAST

The Jurassic Coast, England's only natural World Heritage Site, covers 95 miles (153km) of breathtaking coastline from Devon to Dorset. It was selected by UNESCO, which ranks it alongside other such natural wonders as the Grand Canyon in the US and the Great Barrier Reef in Australia. The area extends from Exmouth to Swanage and the coastline, which is packed with fossils, offers varied examples of landforms, such as the natural arch at Durdle Door and the cove and limestone folding at Lulworth Cove. Briercliffe recommends a tramp along Chesil Beach, a tombolo (sand and shingle spit) which connects the Isle of Portland to Abbotsbury. The highest point of the Jurassic Coast is Golden Cap which is 626ft (191m) tall; here you can also enjoy a centuries-old

CYCLE ROUTE

MAIDEN NEWTON *to* DORCHESTER

DORSET

DISTANCE: 18 MILES (29KM) RETURN TRIP   TIME: 3–4 HOURS

This cycle ride is part of the Sustrans National Route 26 and provides a mix of traffic-free paths and quiet roads that link Maiden Newton to Dorchester. The 9-mile (14km) route is generally flat with a couple of hills to tackle near Dorchester. For those wanting to return to the suggested starting point at Maiden Newton there is the option of cycling back along the route or returning from Dorchester by train.

If you plan to cycle the full 18 miles (29km) to Dorchester and back you should allow around 3 to 4 hours, or more depending on stopping time.

STARTING PLACE

It is suggested that you start at Maiden Newton. If you are arriving by car, park within Maiden Newton and join Route 26 heading south-east towards Dorchester. For those arriving by train you should exit the station and ride into Maiden Newton via Station Road.

THE ROUTE

Starting from Maiden Newton station **[1]**, continue along Station Road until you cycle past the junction with Cattistock Road, then follow Church Road – you are now on National Route 26. When you reach the A356, turn left **[2]** then cycle a short distance before turning right **[3]** into Frome Lane. Keep following the Route 26 signs as the lane turns into a path that takes you alongside the River Frome.

The route takes you through a series of small hamlets – Frome Vauchurch, Cruxton, Notton and Southover. As you approach Southover you revert from bridleway to country lane again **[4]**. When cycling through Southover, those wanting to make a short detour to visit

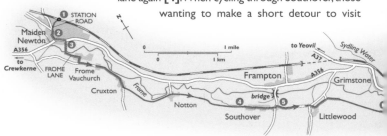

Frampton can use a bridge designed by Sir Christopher Wren to cross the River Frome. Continuing on from Southover, you should follow the Route 26 signs, making sure you turn right to connect to the next section of bridleway **[5]**. This is bumpier than the rest of the route, making this part most suited to mountain bikes or hybrid bikes with wider-rim wheels! The next section of the bridleway route has a tarmac surface and rejoins a country lane through Muckleford **[6]**. You need to go straight on at the crossroads (take care here), then follow the lane to Bradford Peverell **[7]**.

As you arrive in Bradford Peverell you will need to turn left at the staggered crossroads **[8]** and continue to the busy A37. Cross with care **[9]**, then join the shared foot/cycleway and head towards Dorchester. After about half a mile, take the signed left turn through the village of Charminster **[10]**. Approach the centre of the village along West Hill, then take care at the crossroads **[11]** before travelling straight on along East Hill. Follow the road out of the village along Westleaze. The medieval and Elizabethan Wolfeton House is worth a detour here. At the bottom of the hill by the pub, a new traffic-free route takes you over the water meadows **[12]**, and on to Glyde Path Road **[13]**, which takes you into the centre of Dorchester.

Once you enter the town you will be using more heavily trafficked roads, so please take extra care. Dorchester has been inhabited since prehistoric times; there is an Iron Age hill fort south of the town. The Romans called the town Durnovaria and surrounded it with a wall, small segments of which remain. It was the site of numerous insurrections and Judge Jeffreys held his notorious Bloody Assizes in the Oak Room of the Antelope Hotel after the Monmouth rebellion in 1685. Thomas Hardy based the fictional town of Casterbridge on Dorchester and is commemorated in a statue, as is Sir Thomas Hardy, the Flag Captain that Admiral Lord Nelson famously wanted to kiss before his death at Trafalgar. You can return to Maiden Newton by retracing your cycle route or by taking the train from Dorchester West station **[14]**. Please check train times in advance.

landscape of meadows and hedgerows. The 630-mile (1014km) South West Coast Path runs the entire length of the Jurassic Coast from Minehead in Somerset to Old Harry Rocks near the shores of Poole Harbour in Dorset. This is principally a walking trail – just 8 per cent is open to cyclists – but it can be very good to get off the bike for a day's hiking.

The Dorset heathland, immortalized by Thomas Hardy in his novels, once stretched from Dorchester in the west, to the Avon Valley in the east, covering more than 123,553 acres (50,000 hectares). Today, just 17,297 acres (7000 hectares) remain. Heathland is found all across Europe, but worldwide it is a threatened habitat, said to be rarer than the tropical rain forests. The heathland in east Dorset is less populous and short cycle routes cross parts of it – do not miss the opportunity to visit the spectacular, 1,000-year-old Corfe Castle while in the area and learn about its bloodthirsty, troubled past.

ABOVE: Thomas Hardy, pictured here in the early 1920s at his home at Max Gate, east of Dorchester, enjoyed cycling in Dorset.

The Studland Peninsula sits on the west and southern shores of Poole Harbour. Visitors can enjoy woodland, heathland, sandy beaches, sand dunes, bogs and salt marsh. From South Haven Point to the chalk cliffs of Handfast Point and Old Harry Rocks at the eastern end of the Jurassic Coast, is a beautiful 3-mile (5km) long beach behind which lies heathland believed to contain the richest 2,471 acres (1,000 hectares) for wildflowers in the UK. There are many circular rides in the area ranging from 8 to 47 miles (13–76km) and include such areas as Clouds Hill and Studland Beach (be warned: one section is dedicated to naturists). Alternatively, ride through the Rempstone Estate, which has an ancient stone circle, on the Rempstone Ride that runs for 12 miles (19km) between the village of Norden, near Corfe Castle, and Studland or Shell Bay.

THE CROWNING GLORY OF THE ATLANTIC COAST

'The rugged and romantic coast of north Devon was a favourite destination for cyclist Harold Briercliffe who described this coastline as "incomparably the finest and the grandest in the country". I'm following part of his route through Exmoor Forest, taking in wooded ravines and deep valleys, tumbling cliffs and a stunning coastline, including Combe Martin and the port of Ilfracombe.'

CLARE BALDING

Our journey begins in Lynmouth on the north edge of Exmoor, at the foot of a steep-sided valley. Briercliffe, uncharacteristically poetic, describes it as a romantic situation: 'Two hundred yards from the shore the two Lyn streams, East and West, unite and even their final few yards are inclined, so that Lynmouth has no untidy estuary.' The course of the two streams provides some of the most picturesque stretches of valley scenery in the country. Thomas Gainsborough, who honeymooned there, called it 'the most delightful place for a landscape painter this country can boast'. Charming though it is, however, the village is much changed since Harold cycled through here during the late 1940s. On 16 August 1952 it was the scene of the worst post-war flooding disaster in Britain; the village was devastated by the sheer power of nature.

ABOVE: Clare Balding, complete with Harold Briercliffe's bicycle, near Lynmouth on her tour of north Devon's Atlantic coast.

ELECTRIC LIGHT

It is ironic that Lynmouth was destroyed by natural forces in this way because many years earlier the village had built a pioneering hydroelectric power scheme on this river. Incredibly, Lynmouth and Lynton became the first settlements in the UK to have electric lighting in 1890, powered by electric generators on the East

THE LYNMOUTH
DISASTER

During August 1952 North Devon experienced 250 times the normal rainfall for the month. In the 24 hours before the flood some 9in (22cm) of rain fell on Exmoor, just 4 miles (6.5km) away. The rain flowed off the moors and into the East and West Lyn Rivers, which turned into raging torrents as they tore down the valley into Lynmouth. Houses and shops folded up like packs of cards as 90 million tonnes of water swept down the narrow valley – 34 people lost their lives. More than 100 buildings and 28 of the 31 bridges were either destroyed or seriously damaged. A wooden cross, made by one of the survivors, was erected in 2002 in memory of the flood victims on the 50th anniversary of the disaster.

LEFT: A hotel collapses in the severe floods that devastated Lynmouth and killed 34 people in 1952.

DEVON

ABOVE: The original route (in red) taken by Harold Briercliffe in Devon, using a 1940s Ordnance Survey map. His route was the inspiration for Clare Balding's journey through Devon.

Lyn River. They also powered an ice-making machine for the local fishing industry, but all was destroyed in the flood of 1952.

Small-scale hydroelectric power schemes were common in the Exmoor area, but they fell into disuse after the introduction of the National Grid. A new hydroelectric power station was built in 1983 at the Lynmouth Crossroads, where the East and West Lyn Rivers meet. There is also an experimental tidal power scheme off the coast.

The village of Lynton is perched high on top of the gorge above Lynmouth. In the nineteenth century the tall cliffs were a major obstacle to economic development. Both villages relied principally on the sea for transportation because crossing Exmoor was so difficult. Daily essentials were landed at Lynmouth and transported up the hill to Lynton by packhorse or horse and cart. Holiday-makers were visiting as early as the mid-1820s, arriving on paddle steamers from various Bristol Channel ports, but only the bravest would tackle the daunting walk uphill to Lynton. The Cliff Railway provided the solution; it opened in 1890 and is said to be the steepest railway ride in the world.

ABOVE: Clare Balding visits Glen Lyn Gorge, the location of a pioneering experiment in hydroelectric power.

A MUSEUM PIECE

The Cliff Railway, a water-powered funicular railway, was a museum piece when Harold Briercliffe visited the village in the 1940s; 60 years later it's still going. It boasts 862ft (263m) of rail, rising 500ft (152m) feet vertically, at a gradient of 1:1.75 – automatic brakes lock in the case of any mishap. From the railway car, which is civilized enough to transport bicycles, there are glorious views across Lynmouth Bay.

Harold Briercliffe describes Lynton as 'a breezy resort reminiscent of Buxton in its hill-country atmosphere, quite in contrast with the confined air of Lynmouth.' The countryside outside the town wins a high accolade from him: 'climb out of the town westwards, leaving the villas behind, and go through a rocky little gorge into the Valley of the Rocks. This is one of the finest bits of country in the West. The road gives little impression of what lies to the north, closer to the sea.'

THE VALLEY OF THE ROCKS

The Valley of the Rocks is unique in Britain: it runs parallel to the sea rather than inland from it. It is now a dry valley and its extraordinary rugged landscape earned it the popular name of 'Little Switzerland of England'. Harold Briercliffe advised his readers that once here, 'it is necessary to leave the bicycle and to go rightward, over the hill, to the impressive North

LEFT: The Lynton and Lynmouth Cliff Railway, under construction in 1890 and today in full working order with two cars approaching the passing point.

Walk, which gives a panorama of cliff, rocky shore and sea unequalled in the West Country'.

The landscape, unchanged over the centuries bar the odd pay-and-display car park, boasts breathtaking, dizzying views of the surrounding countryside. The biggest rock faces are named: look out for 'Ragged Jack', 'The Devil's Cheese Ring' and 'Castle Rock'. A local legend says that a white lady can be seen on Castle Rock when viewed from a distance.

WOODY BAY RESORT

Back on the bicycle our journey continues through dense woodland to Lee Bay then turns inland, through a series of hairpin bends back out to Woody Bay, a remote and unspoilt corner of North Devon. In 1885 the bay was purchased by Colonel Benjamin Lake, a wealthy solicitor

ABOVE: Clare Balding cycles through The Valley of the Rocks, which Harold describes as 'one of the finest bits of country in the West'.

from Kent, who wanted to develop it as an exclusive resort to rival nearby Lynton and Lynmouth. To this end he built new roads, a railway and a new pier to provide access for tourist steamers. The pier opened in 1897 but bad weather and low tides prevented the first boats from docking. The pier was seriously damaged by storms in 1899 and 1900 and was never repaired. Later that year the colonel was bankrupt and his dream ended. The remains of the pier were demolished in 1902, although remnants of it can still be seen on the shoreline. The railway line closed in 1935, but volunteers reopened a 1-mile (1.6km) section of the Lynton & Barnstaple Railway in 2004, enabling visitors to travel a small part of the original narrow-gauge railway through the Heddon Valley.

Leaving Woody Bay the road turns southwards away from the sea. Stop here at Highveer Point for a striking look-out; Briercliffe describes this stretch

as 'the finest part of the accessible coast of North Devon'. Continue down into Heddon Valley, one of the deepest valleys in England, which runs down to the sea at Heddon's Mouth Beach. Journey on to Combe Martin, a village that consists of a single long road that runs for 2 miles (3km) down to the sea.

Silver was mined in Combe Martin as early as the thirteenth century and there are items within the Crown Jewels collection made from Combe silver. There are several disused silver mines close to the village; the last one closed in 1890, but enthusiasts have been exploring old mine workings since 1999. Architects have also found what they believe to be a twelfth-century monastic grange – complete with hemp mill and hemp pool – where the stems of the hemp plant were used to make a rough cloth and cord.

ILFRACOMBE PORT

'Onwards from Combe Martin the road is smoother and less hilly,' notes Briercliffe. 'It skirts Sandy Bay and the long promontory called Barrow Nose. Still winding picturesquely between the hills and the sea and occasionally going inland up short dales, it reaches the pretty bay of Hele, and climbs through a low pass before dropping into Ilfracombe, the largest seaside resort of Devon.' The town has been settled since the Ice Age and was mentioned in the Domesday Book. It played a significant role in the nation's defences; in 1208 it was listed as providing King John with ships and men to invade Ireland; in 1247 it dispatched a ship with the fleet that was sent to conquer the Western Isles of Scotland and it sent a ship to support the siege of Calais in 1346. Ilfracombe was an important port in the fourteenth century; Briercliffe maintained it was a greater port than Liverpool, offering a safe natural harbour off the stormy Bristol Channel.

The novelist, diarist and playwright Fanny Burney stayed in the resort in 1817 and recorded an action-packed visit, including an escape after being cut off by the tide, two ships in distress in a storm and a captured Spanish ship in the harbour. In the 1820s Welsh miners were employed to dig four tunnels to the beaches to give access by horse-drawn carriage; prior to this visitors had to make their way around the coast on foot at low tide.

Harold damns the town perhaps with faint praise: 'there is still a harbour, but the town is almost entirely modern', suggesting perhaps that the resort may well have been suffering from a decline in tourism and industry in the 1940s. However, it presents an interesting contradictory face to the visitor; while it clutches on to the old seaside attractions, and still pays homage to its stunning Atlantic views, it is also home to cutting-edge artist Damien Hirst's award-winning restaurant and bar. The town appears to be rising out of the ashes of its many fires into a dynamic future.

While tourism is important in North Devon, its inhabitants have learned to their cost that the landscape cannot always be bent to their will. It remains at heart a wild, romantic and rugged region.

ABOVE: A 1950s view of the popular seaside resort of Ilfracombe taken from the heights of Hillsborough Hill, site of an Iron Age fortress.

CENTRAL ENGLAND

*'It is a stimulating experience to stand on the hills
north of Eyam (The Peak District plague village) and
look westward across the limestone upland, undulating
in smooth, stone-walled surges'* Harold Briercliffe

The village of Meriden in the green belt between Coventry and Birmingham is traditionally regarded as the heart of the UK, though purists argue that the actual point is located in farmland 18 miles (29km) to the north-east. A pillar commemorating the village's exalted position has been in place for at least 200 years – some say 500 years. Appropriately, Meriden is also home to a memorial to all the cyclists who died in the First World War. Twenty thousand cyclists attended the unveiling on 21 May 1921 and many gather for an annual ceremony to pay their respects.

ABOVE: A signpost highlights the village of Meriden's position slap-bang in the centre of England.
PAGE 89: A Scottish undergraduate cycles through Oxford in full regalia in 1939.

THE MIDLANDS

The Midlands, long a hive of industry, is also home to great tracts of beautiful countryside. Despite Briercliffe's viewpoint that 'in the Midlands there are no adequate topographical compensations for the absence of ocean,' there is much to please the visitor. Warwickshire has open fields to the south and the forest of Arden to the north. Enjoy the preserved prettiness of Stratford-upon-Avon, home of William Shakespeare, and the magnificence of Warwick Castle. To the extreme west is the fertile county of Shropshire with its many wonderful manor houses and some beautiful cycle routes. The Peak District of Derbyshire offers challenging, rugged magnificence, Nottinghamshire has Sherwood Forest and the beautiful Clumber Park for day trips. To the south is the lovely flat, rolling farmland of Leicestershire and Northamptonshire, which is studded with pretty villages. To the west are the fertile fields of the Vale of Evesham, famous for its fruit, and the fertile beauty of Hereford and Worcester. The Marches define the area where England meets the border of Wales. It is littered with ruined castles, symbols of centuries of conflict between the two countries. Running north–south along the Welsh border is Offa's Dyke Path, now a national trail that takes you through some truly spectacular scenery. The Malvern Hills, a designated Area of Outstanding Natural Beauty, crosses three county borders and is home to a range of landscapes, making it a paradise for bird watchers.

Bracing east winds rush across the Lincolnshire coastline, home to numerous stalwart seaside resorts such as Cleethorpes, Mablethorpe and Skegness, the town with the infamous tag *it's so bracing*. Much further south is Boston, once an important port before the Wash silted up, making it inaccessible to large vessels. Inland is the beautiful, but tiny, city of Lincoln.

To the south are the Cotswolds, Gloucestershire and Oxfordshire, whose charm and beauty attract millions of visitors a year. The Cotswold hills offer the picture-postcard vision of England with undulating countryside and pretty, honey-coloured cottages. To the south and west is the magnificent Forest of Dean, one of the few remaining ancient forests in England. Below the River Severn are the flat plains of the Severn Valley, which are perfect for cycling. Visit Gloucester Cathedral where the young Henry III was crowned with his mother's bracelet in 1216. Oxfordshire, with its gentle rolling hills, is lovely cycling country. Visit Blenheim Palace, one of the most exquisite stately homes in the country, or explore Oxford itself, a city packed with history yet not preserved in aspic, for despite the ancient and beautiful college buildings and its air of gentrified intelligence, it retains a lively sense of modernity.

ABOVE: The Stratford Greenway cycle route winds its way through some very pretty Warwickshire countryside on a disused railway line.

THE MARCHES

The Marches lie between the river valleys of England and the mountains of Wales. The area is Anglo-Welsh and much of it lies in the English counties of Shropshire, Herefordshire, Worcestershire and Gloucestershire, which run along

WOODHALL SPA
Circular Route

LINCOLNSHIRE

DISTANCE: 16 MILES (25KM) TIME: 2 HOURS

This quiet and flat circular route of around 16 miles (25km) passes through unique woodlands and heathland as well as the attractive village of Woodhall Spa. The village was developed after John Parkinson accidentally uncovered a spring when hunting for coal in 1821. In its Edwardian heyday the spa attracted royalty and high society. The village is also famous for its association with 617 Squadron, the 'Dambusters', which operated out of an RAF site near the village for the last 18 months of the war. There are a number of aircraft heritage sites in the vicinity and the village has a small cottage museum. This route should take around 2 hours to complete, or more if you stop at places along the way.

STARTING PLACES

The suggested starting place is in the centre of Woodhall Spa. If you are arriving by car there is a car park in the centre of the village on Station Road. Those arriving by car could also start their circular route at any of the small settlements along the way. Wherever you

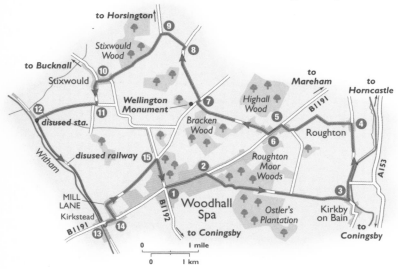

start, it would be best to travel anti-clockwise, particularly if you are cycling with children, to minimize the number of right turns at junctions.

THE ROUTE FROM WOODHALL SPA

Leave the car park on Station Road [1] and continue along Station Road and The Broadway in the direction of Mareham. You should pass the Golf Hotel then turn right when you see the turning for Kirkby on Bain [2]. Follow this road out of Woodhall Spa and on past Roughton Moor Woods on your left and Ostler's Plantation on the right. The plantation is on the site of an RAF air base that was a key part of Britain's air defences during the Second World War. Conifers and oaks were planted around the airbase after the war but plenty of signs of the base still remain.

Continuing on from the plantation you reach a T-junction where you should follow the left turn to Roughton [3]. This part of the route is flat and straight and you should arrive at Roughton without delay. You should then turn left following the sign for Woodhall Spa [4]. At the next T-junction [5] you should turn left again, still following the sign for Woodhall Spa, then turn right following the sign for Horsington [6]. This road takes you away from Woodhall Spa once again with views across to Highall Wood on the right and Bracken Wood on the left. After about 1 mile (1.6km) you will reach a staggered crossroads. At this point you could take time to look at the monument to the Duke of Wellington, a bust on a granite obelisk. The woodland behind the monument was grown from acorns planted in commemoration immediately after the Battle of Waterloo. At the crossroads you should turn right then immediately left as signed for Horsington [7].

You should turn left at both of the next two junctions [8] [9] before cycling on a straight section of road alongside Stixwould Wood. This 'limewood' is owned and managed by the Forestry Commission and contains the most important example of small-leaved lime woodland in Britain.

Past the lime woodland you will reach Stixwould where you should turn right for Bucknall then left for Stixwould station [10]. At the next T-junction you should turn right [11] and head for the former Stixwould Station. Here you should turn left through the car park and join the Water Rail Way path [12]. This old railway line now provides a quiet traffic-free path for cyclists and walkers alongside the River Withem and is part of National Cycle Network route 1. You should cycle along this path for about 1½ miles (2.4km) until you go under the bridge at Woodhall, then you should turn left to leave the old railway line [13]. Turn right at the T-junction then left along Mill Lane [14]. At the next crossroads you should turn right [15] following the signs for Woodhall Spa. This takes you back to your starting point on Station Road.

the border of Wales. King Offa of Mercia constructed the first barricade along the border, a dyke, late in the eighth century and the Normans constructed a string of motte-and-bailey castles to help contain and control the Welsh. Offa's Dyke, the UK's longest ancient monument, is a linear earthwork designed to present an open view into Wales. While much of its 80-mile (129km) route can be explored on foot via the 177-mile (285km) Offa's Dyke National Trail, only short sections can be cycled; however, if you are in the area this spectacle should not be missed. There are also some lovely Forestry Commission cycle trails in the Clun Valley, where some of the best-preserved sections of the dyke can be seen.

Running parallel to Offa's Dyke is the less well-known Wat's Dyke, which was built by Offa's predecessor Aethelbald. It runs from Basingwerk Abbey in Flintshire in the northern Welsh Marches to Maesbury in Shropshire. At points it is only a few yards away from Offa's Dyke: the furthest distance

ABOVE: The Offa's Dyke Path runs the length of the Marches from Chepstow to Prestatyn, but only small sections of it can be cycled.

between the two earthworks is just less than 3 miles (5km). A path for walkers follows the route, but cyclists can reach it via some of the quiet Shropshire country lanes. There are five National Cycle Routes that pass through Shropshire. The Six Castles Cycleway runs from Shrewsbury to Leominster and takes in some magnificent buildings along the way, including Stokesay Castle, one of the finest fortified manor houses in England, and the eleventh-century Ludlow Castle, where Henry VIII's older brother Arthur brought his new wife Catherine of Aragon. Cycle out to Wenlock Edge, a limestone escarpment, from the village of Craven Arms near Stokesay to Much Wenlock. The escarpment was created 400 million years ago, when Shropshire was sited just south of the equator, and is packed with fossils and covered with woodland.

ABOVE: The Cannop Valley Family Cycle Trail is a traffic-free route through the Forest of Dean along the old Severn & Wye railway line.

Between the rivers Severn and Wye lies the ancient Forest of Dean, which covers more than 35 square miles (90 sq km). Briercliffe comments: 'The interests of the Forest are less sophisticated than those of the valley, and there is more serene enjoyment for the cyclist who loves the quieter ways.' It contains both deciduous and evergreen trees with a high quotient of oak, sweet chestnut and beech. Forestry and charcoal provided work for centuries and, at the Clearwell Caverns, iron ore and ochre pigment were mined for more than 4500 years. There is a 10-mile (17km) circular family cycle route that takes you through the heart of the forest, forest tracks and off-road routes for mountain bikers as well as plenty of quiet country lanes and gentle hills. To the north of the forest is Symonds Yat, a scenic viewpoint some 394ft (120m) above the River Wye on the Gloucester side. The Peregrine Path runs from Monmouth to Symonds Yat and follows the River Wye for 3 miles (5km).

The Golden Valley of the River Dore is in south-west Herefordshire, the Black Mountains sit to the west and Hay-on-Wye to the north. It was formed by the same glacier that gouged out the River Wye. The area is renowned for its tranquil beauty, fertile farmland and fruitful orchards. A beautiful cycle ride, which incorporates the Peregrine Path mentioned above, is the Herefordshire Three Rivers Circular Cycle Route, an 85-mile (137km) route that links the rivers Wye, Monnow and Dore.

THE MALVERN HILLS

The Malvern Hills are just 9 miles (14.5km) long and run north–south with a single bare ridge of peaks along the top. They rise 1,395ft (425m) above the Severn Valley to their highest point, Worcestershire Beacon. The hills, which are located in Worcestershire, Herefordshire and a small section of Gloucestershire, are famous for their mineral water and springs.

The hills contain a range of landscapes and habitats over a compact area, with enclosed and unenclosed common, rolling pastures, hedgerow, arable farmland and ancient woodland. It is this combination of environments that makes the Malvern Hills a paradise for birdwatchers, as many different species can be seen in a relatively small area. Buzzards are easy to spot, but goshawks, hobbies, red kites and peregrine falcons can occasionally be seen.

The line down the spine of the hills traditionally formed the county border between Herefordshire and Worcestershire and was an excellent defensive stronghold. Running along the summit is the Shire Dyke, which may have been constructed in the late Bronze Age. On the summit of the Herefordshire Beacon, or 'British Camp', are the remains of an Iron Age hill fort. In addition a Norman motte castle that crowns British Camp is visible for miles around, an imposing symbol of Norman lordship. Beacons have been lit along the spine of the hills since Norman times and on most days the three cathedrals of Hereford, Worcester and Gloucester can be seen. There are some very pretty cycle routes around the country lanes in the foothills of the Malverns and there is plenty of off-road riding on bridleways through the hills; maps are available from Worcestershire County Council and Tourist Information Centres.

ABOVE: Dawn breaks over Shire Ditch and Worcestershire Beacon on a frosty morning in the Malvern Hills.

MALVERN
WATER

The Malvern area has a history of human settlement, possibly because of the purity of its water. Groundwater infiltrates the igneous rock on the hills via faults and fissures until it reaches less permeable sedimentary rocks from which it eventually emerges as a spring. The first water-cure establishment opened in Great Malvern in 1842; Dickens and Darwin both visited. There are more than 100 springs and wells in the region, but only six still supply pure spring water.

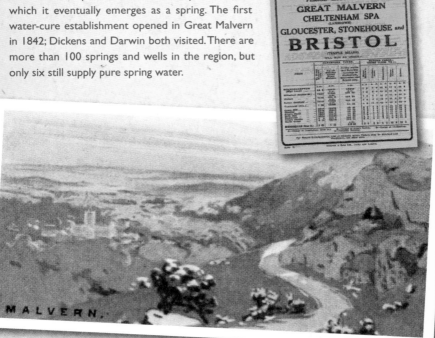

LMS
LONDON MIDLAND AND SCOTTISH RAILWAY

AUTUMN HOLIDAYS

On FRIDAY, SEPTEMBER 24th, 1926, and
Every Friday until October 29th, inclusive
COOK'S
PERIOD EXCURSIONS TO

GREAT MALVERN
CHELTENHAM SPA
(LANSDOWN)
GLOUCESTER, STONEHOUSE and
BRISTOL
(TEMPLE MEADS)
WILL RUN AS UNDER:

MALVERN.

ABOVE: A cigarette card from the 1920s with an idyllic view of Malvern. Originally issued to stiffen the packets, the beautifully designed cards are now valuable collectibles. A pamphlet from 1926 advertises Cook's excursions to Malvern, Cheltenham and Bristol from the Midlands.

THE COTSWOLDS AND STRATFORD-UPON-AVON

To the south are the Cotswolds in the north-west of the county of Oxfordshire, a patchwork of undulating fields, cut through with streams and intercepted by chocolate-box villages, beautiful stereotypes of English rural dwellings. The area has been prosperous since the Middle Ages, when wool was England's chief source of revenue. There are a number of interesting cycle runs out of the city of Oxford that will take you to such sights as the Uffington White Horse, which is situated between the boundaries of southern Oxfordshire and Berkshire. It is thought to be the oldest hill figure in the country; it dates from the Bronze Age and is estimated to be around 3000 years of age. The 374ft (110m) long figure is best viewed from a distance of 3–4 miles (5–6.5km), but on a good day can be seen from 20 miles (32km) away. Alternatively, twitchers should cycle out to Otmoor, a semi-wetland landscape large parts of which are an RSPB reserve.

Moving north into Warwickshire, Stratford-upon-Avon is an essential place to visit and it is easy to cycle round all the historic buildings. A number of cycle routes take you out into the surrounding countryside, including the Stratford Greenway, a 5-mile (8km) cycle route along a disused railway line. Cycle out to

BELOW A photo by Harold Briercliffe of his wife during their cycling tours together. Mrs Briercliffe cycles near The Tower Gateway of Edgehill Castle in Warwickshire

Shottery to visit Ann Hathaway's birthplace or go further east and follow the Battlefields Trail, large chunks of which can be done by bike, out to Edgehill where the first battle of the Civil War took place in 1642. Going just 8 miles (13km) further east across Warwickshire you will find the magnificent fourteenth-century Warwick Castle and nearby the ruins of Kenilworth Castle.

THE PEAK DISTRICT

The Peak District, situated in Staffordshire and Derbyshire, is estimated to attract around 22 million visitors per year yet is still famed for its remote beauty. It is situated at the south end of the Pennine anticline and marks a distinct change in the landscape from the rolling farmland to the south. Its geology divides the area into three characteristic landscapes: the limestone of the White Peak, the rugged rocky outcrops and moorland of the Dark Peak, where cycling is tougher, and the lower hills and valleys of the South West Peak. Harold Briercliffe observed: 'Perhaps no county in England has as much to show in natural phenomena as Derbyshire.' Most of the area falls within the Peak District National Park, which covers 555 square miles (1438 sq km). Briercliffe, who clearly relished a two-wheeled challenge, rated it as providing sufficient interest for a week or fortnight's tour.

Vast swathes of the area are uplands (more than 1,000ft/305m above sea level). The highest point is Kinder Scout, at 2,087ft (636m) tall. In April 1932 a mass trespass took place in what is known as the Battle of Kinder Scout, which highlighted the local desire to walk freely on moor and mountain. The landscape, despite its name, does not produce sharp peaks, but gritstone escarpments and rounded hills. Here there is rough pasture, heather moorland and blanket bog. Woodland forms less than eight per cent of the park: broad-leaved woods in the dales of the White Peak and conifer plantations around the fringes of reservoirs. The weather is changeable; in winter the roads can be closed by snow and soaking rain and dense mist can suddenly descend at any time of the year.

The area of the Dark Peak almost surrounds the White Peak. It is made up of vast areas of moorland and pocketed with blanket bog. The highest points of the Peak District are located here and include Kinder Scout, Bleaklow Plateau and Black Hill. Water pours from the heights and some 50 valleys have been flooded to form reservoirs, including the Upper Derwent Valley, which contains Ladybower, Derwent and Howden

CYCLE ROUTE

KING'S SUTTON to MARSTON ST LAWRENCE

NORTHAMPTONSHIRE

DISTANCE: 17 MILES (27KM)   TIME: 2–3 HOURS

This is a quiet circular route of around 17 miles (27km) following a series of scenic country lanes between idyllic villages, starting and finishing in King's Sutton – which was mentioned in the Domesday Book of 1086 – and going via Marston St Lawrence, whose church dates back to 1100. The route is hilly in places and should take about 2 to 3 hours to cycle, or more if you stop along the way.

STARTING PLACES

The suggested starting place for those planning to arrive by train is at King's Sutton station. If you are arriving by car there is a car park at the station and plenty of on-street parking within King's Sutton. Those arriving by car could also start their circular route at any of the other villages along the way. Wherever you start, it would be best to travel anti-clockwise along the route, particularly if you are cycling with children, to minimize the number of right turns at junctions.

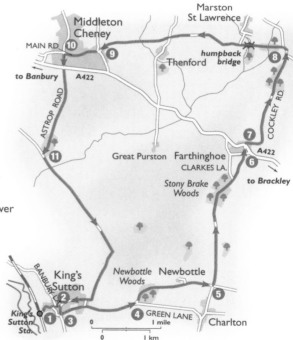

THE ROUTE FROM KING'S SUTTON

At the railway station car park **[1]** follow the access road. Pass Banbury Lane on your left then turn right, following the road sign for Charlton **[2]**. Go up Whittall Street until you reach the open square and take the left turn along Astrop Road **[3]**. Follow Astrop Road out of the village, passing the recreation ground on your left then climbing up the hill towards Charlton. Turn left when you see the road sign for Newbottle **[4]**. The road continues to rise as it passes through Newbottle Woods with stunning views of King's Sutton and beyond to the west. You will pass a turning on the left to Newbottle. This interesting hamlet also features in the Domesday Book and once had a population of some 200 inhabitants. In the Middle Ages the owner of the manor enclosed the surrounding fields and moved the population to nearby Charlton. Today Newbottle has a population of just 14 and there is only a small group of buildings including the manor, church and former vicarage. However, it is still possible to see the outline of where the original houses stood.

Continuing on from Newbottle, you reach a crossroads where you should turn left and follow the sign for Farthinghoe **[5]**. The journey to Farthinghoe is along a generally straight road that drops down a hill and passes under the canopy of Stony Brake Woods. As you reach Farthinghoe, ignore the left turn along Clarkes Lane and head straight on until you reach the crossroads with Queens Street and Charlton Way **[6]**. The safest and most convenient way of negotiating your way through the village is to dismount and walk straight across into the short one-way section of Charlton Way, then remount and cycle to the pedestrian crossing over the busy A422 **[7]**. Here you should again dismount to use the crossing, then get back on your bicycle to continue out of the village along Cockley Road.

The next part of the route includes more attractive views as you wind you way through a patchwork of fields and a wood. Shortly after the wood there is a turning to the right, which you should ignore. Instead take the first turn on the left, which is along a weight-restricted narrow lane **[8]**. This passes through another wood then over a humpback bridge, which offers a stunning view across a lake. At the next junction you should turn left. This road takes you past the left turn for Thenford and into Middleton Cheney via a traffic-calmed road. When you reach the junction with Main Road **[9]** you will need to turn right (take care) and travel for around ½ mile (0.8km) along Main Road until you see a left turn for King's Sutton **[10]**.

Take the left turn towards King's Sutton along Astrop Road. This is a quiet route out of Middleton Cheney with views across open countryside towards Banbury. Astrop Road takes you down a hill until you reach a T-junction **[11]**. Turn left here and you are now on the final leg of the journey. The road takes you through open countryside up a hill then down into King's Sutton. Make your way along Richmond Street then down the hill until you reach the junction with Whittall Street. From this point you can follow the signs back to the station.

reservoirs, where sandpipers, goshawks and mergansers can be seen. This area offers challenging cycling and principally attracts mountain bikers. However, there are wonderful roads through the valleys for tourers. Briercliffe describes it as, 'second only, in England, to the Lake District as a pass-storming area'. There are many cycle rental shops in the area and if you find the idea of a day's touring attractive then why not rent a mountain bike and give yourself a taste of seriously tough cycling, or do some hiking.

The White Peak covers the area in the south and centre of the Peak District. It forms the much-eroded dome of the limestone plateau. This is cut by steep-sided valleys, or dales, and is criss-crossed by dry-stone walls that shine out silver white in the summer sun. The limestone has been eroded by acid rain to form spectacular caves, notably around the Castleton area of Hope Valley, where the limestone meets the grit and shale of the Dark Peak. The Peak Cavern – or Devil's Arse as it is otherwise known – is the largest natural cave entrance in the UK. Blue John and Treak Cliff caverns are the only source of semi-precious fluorite in the UK, a rare mineral known as Blue John. The area has long been inhabited – the stone circle and henge of Arbor Low near Youlgreave has been dubbed the 'Stonehenge of the North'.

The most famous dale in this area is Dove Dale, otherwise known as Little Switzerland, which lies north of Ashbourne and attracts an estimated 2 million visitors a year. The River Dove carved its way through the limestone plateau creating a spectacular gorge famous for its spires, arches, rock pinnacles and caves. It is beautiful and worth a visit, though it is not great for cycling and hellish on a Sunday when it is packed with visitors. Running parallel to Dove Dale is Manifold Valley. The River Manifold disappears underground here and there, and there are caverns and potholes. Near the village of Whetton, 260ft (80m) above the valley floor, is the natural cavern Thor's Cave. The entrance is a symmetrical arch 33ft (10m) high

ABOVE: A cyclist pedals alongside Derwent Reservoir in the Peak District. The water, 3 miles by 1 mile (5 × 1.6km), is surrounded by wooded hills.

and 25ft (7.5m) wide and it can easily be reached by the Manifold Way.

The South West Peak is a mixture of wild heather moorland on the hilltops where grouse shooting takes place. Some hilltops have gritstone ridges such as can be seen at Ramshaw Rocks or the Roaches. The valleys are filled with hay meadows and sweet pasture divided by gritstone walls.

There are numerous lovely cycle routes in the White Peak and South West Peak area. The Manifold Way offers about 9 miles (14.5km) of almost traffic-free cycling. The Tissington Trail runs through the heart of the White Peak from Ashbourne to Parsley Hay and links with the wonderful 17½ mile (28km) High Peak Trail, which runs from High Peak Junction to Parsley Hay. The

ABOVE: A 1960s photo of a couple admiring the view from Thorpe Cloud, a 900-ft (274m) tall limestone hill at the southern end of Dovedale.

Monsal Trail starts at Wye Dale and follows much of the route of an old railway track alongside the River Wye for about 12 miles (20km), ending up near Bakewell. Only the eastern part of this trail is suitable for bicycles, however; parts of the western section are tough going even for walkers.

THE PENNINE BRIDLEWAY

The start of the Pennine Way, which opened in 1965, is in Edale, but this is strictly for walkers. The Pennine Bridleway, however, is open to both cyclists and riders. The High Peak Trail is part of this route, which runs roughly parallel with the Pennine Way from the Peak District in Derbyshire via the Yorkshire Dales and on up to Northumberland National Parks using a mix of pack-horse trails, drove roads, disused railway lines and newly created bridleways. Its southernmost point is at Middleton Top, near where it heads north on the Cromford and the High Peak Trail mentioned above.

SHERWOOD FOREST

Nottinghamshire lies to the east of the Peak District. To the south of the county is the industrial city of Nottingham, while to the north and west old coalfields are undergoing green regeneration. In the north-west of the county is the legendary Sherwood Forest. Five hundred acres (202 hectares) of ancient woodland have been preserved and form part of Sherwood Forest Country Park. Cycle routes run through the heart of the forest. There are 900 ancient oak trees here, the most notable of which is the Major Oak, thought to be 800 years old, weighing 23 tons and with a trunk circumference of 33ft (10m). According to local legend its hollow trunk was used as a hideout by Robin Hood's men. Sustrans National Cycle Route 6 runs from Nottingham through Sherwood Forest and moves on to Rotherham and Sheffield. Clumber Park offers 3,800 acres (1537 hectares) of woodland, heath and rolling farmland, which is riddled with lovely cycle routes, both long and short, and linked to Sherwood Forest by National Cycle Routes. It was once the site of a magnificent house but the chapel and walled kitchen garden are all that remain, along with Europe's longest avenue of lime trees at the entrance.

ABOVE: An early twentieth-century illustration with a dashing depiction of the legendary Robin Hood with Maid Marian and his Merry Men.

Charnwood Forest, once densely wooded, is now a landscape of open heath, woodland and rocky outcrops thought to date back 600 million years. It covers around 30 square miles (78 sq km) and is situated in north Leicestershire. There is good cycling in the forest that takes you around and not over the rocky ridges. Beacon Hill is home to a towering plinth that marks its summit. On a clear day the hills of the Peak District and the spire of Lincoln Cathedral can be seen from the top. Bardon Hill is the highest point but you have to walk up to the top.

THE BATTLE
OF BOSWORTH

The Battle of Bosworth Field took place in 1485 and was the last occasion when an English king was killed in the field. The Wars of the Roses finally ended when Richard III lost his life and Henry VII was crowned as the first Tudor monarch. For more than 200 years it was believed that the battle took place on Albion Hill, but four years of intensive research have revealed that the site of the battle was near the village of Stoke Golding, some two miles from Albion Hill. The exact location is yet to be revealed because of fears that treasure hunters could remove valuable evidence.

ABOVE: The Battle of Bosworth Field was fought on 22 August 1485 and was the penultimate battle of the Wars of the Roses. This illustration features Henry Tudor's army advancing to meet Richard III on the eve of the battle.

Moving east the Lincolnshire countryside flattens out. However, Lincoln itself sits on a hill, with its honey-coloured gothic cathedral erected between the twelfth and fourteenth centuries, perched on top like an ecclesiastical cake decoration. Its spire rises to 265 ft (81 metres) and can be seen from two miles (3.2km) away. William the Conqueror built a fortress here, as did the Romans before him. The city has tiny, steep, cobbled streets, lined with medieval houses; it is also home to the earliest examples of 12th-century domestic architecture found in the UK. A 25-mile (40km) circular cycle route, The Water Rail Way, runs through open fenland landscapes and links Lincoln to Sustrans Cycle Route 1 (Dover to John o' Groats), the eastern section of which runs for 195 miles (314km) from Hull in Yorkshire through the pretty, undulating countryside of the Lincolnshire Wolds and through the fens, down to Fakenham, just inland from the north Norfolk coast. The Water Rail Way is dotted with beautiful sculptures and passes close to Tattershall Castle, a fortified and moated red-brick tower built in the fifteenth century and used as a look-out during the Napoleonic Wars.

In Rutland, the Rutland Water Cycleway is a stunning 22-mile (35km) cycle route built through woods and around the edges of one of England's largest man-made lakes, Rutland Water, a regular home to 20,000 waterfowl. Ospreys can be seen fishing over the reservoir between April and September. Drop down to the 82-arch, ¾-mile (1.2km) long Harringworth Viaduct, the longest in Britain.

The 16-mile (26km) Belvoir Route is partially rough, and tough going in parts, but offers wonderful views of the countryside and of the exquisite nineteenth-century Belvoir Castle. The house and gardens are open to the public, but opening times change according to the season and it is not open daily so check before visiting. The whole county is dotted with pretty villages such as Stamford, famous for its Georgian buildings, which frequently feature in costume dramas.

Northamptonshire has some beautiful cycle routes running through the countryside. Visit the Bluebell Line cycle route in spring when it is at its prettiest; the 20-mile (32km) route begins and ends in the market town of Daventry. The Brampton Valley Way connects Market Harborough and Northampton on a traffic-free route and takes you through the dark drama of Great Oxendon tunnel – a 1,358ft (414m) disused railway tunnel – you will need a flashlight. This links with the Midshires Way – a 225 mile (362km) footpath and intermittent bridleway that runs from Bledlow in Buckinghamshire to Stockport across the counties. Cycling access in the Derbyshire section is poor, so check your route carefully before attempting the full journey.

CLARE EXPLORES THE TIMELESS COTSWOLDS

'It's easy to see why the beauty of the Cotswolds is so appealing to visitors from across the world. There's something so relaxing in regarding these gently rolling hills — or wolds — and picking out the church spires and soft yellow stone of the sleepy villages. But is there more to this area than meets the eye?'

CLARE BALDING

Millions of visitors are drawn to the Cotswolds every year to enjoy what is popularly regarded as quintessential English countryside all dotted with immaculate, chocolate-box villages. The Cotswolds appear to be preserved in aspic, offering an idyllic view of our past.

The Cotswolds are an affluent part of the UK, a position maintained since the development of the wool trade in the Middle Ages. Harold Briercliffe describes them as 'bare uplands, not greatly appealing in themselves but holding

ABOVE: Clare Balding reads one of Harold Briercliffe's *Cycling Touring Guides* in the Cotswolds, an area he describes as 'lovely and varied'.

in their folds exquisite valleys and much splendid domestic architecture.' The Cotswolds are the largest designated Area of Outstanding Natural Beauty in England and Wales; 85,000 people live here, most in tiny communities of fewer than 300.

BROADWAY – THE JEWEL OF THE COTSWOLDS

Harold Briercliffe toured the area extensively, urging his readers not to neglect the lesser-known areas, including Fairford, Brill and Chipping Norton. Our journey begins in Broadway, a village known as the 'Jewel of the Cotswolds' or the 'Show Village of England'. It is famous for its broad main street, one of the longest in Britain and for its quaintness. It was not altogether to Briercliffe's taste: 'The prettiness and trimness seem to be overdone – and there is more than a little unnecessary artifice about it all: like a pretty woman who has made up rather too well.' Certainly Broadway is so impossibly perfect that it almost feels like a film set, there's not so much as a scrap of litter to sully the image. Tourism is the lifeblood of the Cotswolds but there may be a price to pay for all this attention.

BROADWAY

THE COTSWOLDS

BELOW: The original route (in red) taken by Harold Briercliffe in the Cotswolds, using a 1940s Ordnance Survey map.

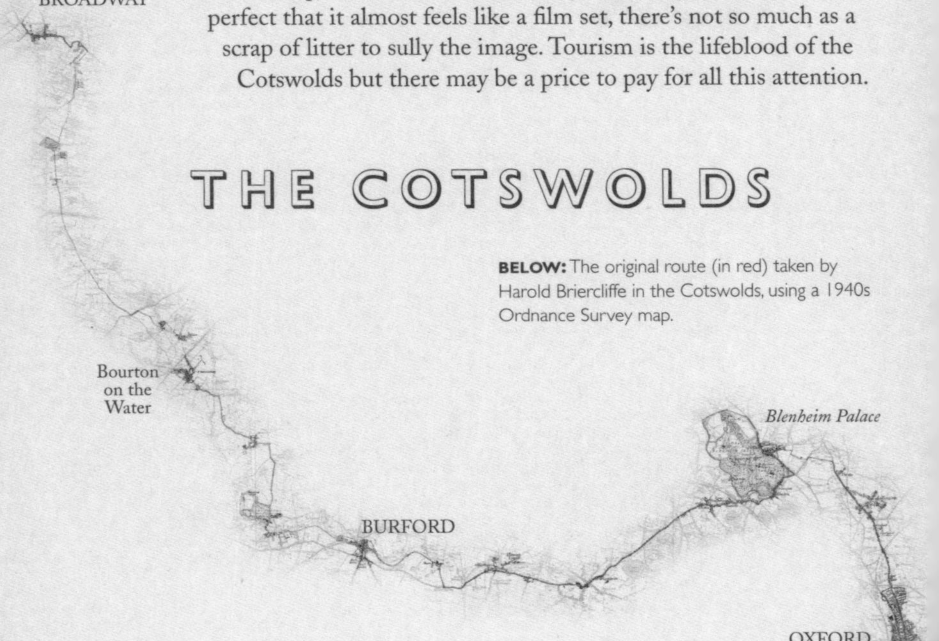

Bourton
on the
Water

Blenheim Palace

BURFORD

OXFORD

ARTS AND CRAFTS

Broadway Tower, an eighteenth-century folly, designed by James Wyatt and completed in 1798, was built to resemble a castle. One of its most famous occupants was William Morris, the designer, architect, poet and champion of the Arts and Crafts Movement; he used it as a holiday retreat with his friends Edward Burne-Jones and Dante Gabriel Rossetti. The Tower's Morris Room commemorates his passion for nature and the important role he played in preserving the distinctive nature of the Cotswolds. He founded the Society for the Protection of Ancient Buildings in 1877 as a practical protest against a scheme to 'restore' Tewkesbury Abbey (when visiting the tower, look out for a poignant memorial to an A.W. 38 Whitley bomber that crashed there during training in 1943).

ABOVE: 'Here, at an altitude of 1,024ft [312m], there is a tower, built in 1798, and from it the eye ranges over a panorama as varied as it is beautiful', wrote Harold Briercliffe of Broadway Tower.

Moving out of Broadway the cyclist can tackle Fish Hill, at 1,026ft (312m) the highest point of the northern end of the Cotswold Hills. The skyline is dominated by Broadway Tower from which you can view the immense panorama of Cotswold countryside stretched out before you in a 360-degree radius: 'Beyond Bredon Hill, in the middle distance, rise the ridges of the Malvern hills and in the north-west the hump of The Wrekin, (a hill in east Shropshire), can sometimes be sighted. In spring, the vale below is fleecy with orchard blossom,' says Briercliffe. Part of Harold Briercliffe's success was in highlighting quirky local features. Broadway Tower is one such example – the views are phenomenal. From here one can see that the countryside looks just as it did half a century ago; the pattern of the fields, the hedgerows, they're all still there.

ABOVE: Clare Balding enjoys the view from the top of Broadway Tower. The Cotswold sunsets are magical from this vantage point.

The journey continues through Upper Slaughter, a village built on the side of a hill and on to nearby Lower Slaughter: 'A stream flows down the street between the cottages and here and there are bridges across the water,' notes Briercliffe. Half a mile east of Lower Slaughter is the Fosse Way, a Roman road that crosses England in a straight line for 182 miles (292km) linking Exeter and Lincoln and which has been in use as a main thoroughfare for 2,000 years. Because it runs along busy A-roads, only small sections of the Fosse Way are suitable for relaxed cycling; please check routes on an Ordnance Survey map.

MODEL SIZE

Harold, ever the rebel, was not affected by such limitations and followed the route to Bourton-on-the-Water, which he describes as one of the most engaging of the larger villages in the Cotswolds: 'A stream flows down the main street, through lawns, and is crossed by ornamental bridges. Behind the New Inn, at the south-east corner of the village stands a model of Bourton on a scale of one-tenth. This is an unusual and faithful reproduction.' It's a reproduction that can still be enjoyed today. Even the scale reproduction has a scale model of itself – like something out of *Alice in Wonderland*, going on for infinity.

The journey continues to Burford, which Harold describes as, 'one of the best preserved old towns in England, and one of the most picturesque'. Burford was in Britain's industrial heartland in the Middle Ages and provided the wool for half of all the cloth produced in England. A literal translation of the word Cotswolds is

RIGHT: A 1937 photograph of Bourton-on-the-Water, called 'The Little Venice of The Cotswolds' because of the number of bridges that link one side of the village to the other.

BELOW: Clare Balding surveys the scene from the same bridge seventy years later.

BURFORD AND THE
REVOLTING LEVELLERS

The River Windrush runs along the valley floor in Burford. Nearby is the twelfth-century St John the Baptist church, which Briercliffe describes as having a Norman west door and several fine chapels. He does not refer to the Burford Levellers, a surprising omission. After the execution of Charles I in 1649, two breakaway divisions of the Parliamentary army marched from Salisbury to Banbury calling for political and social reform. They were intercepted by Cromwell at Burford and the church was pressed into use as a prison. For three days, 340 disaffected prisoners were incarcerated there. One of the men, an Anthony Sedley, carved his name on the font and this can still be seen today. The three ringleaders were shot in the churchyard – the bullet holes can still be seen. Later Cromwell addressed the mutineers from the pulpit. The ideas of the Levellers, and those who died at Burford, are commemorated annually on Levellers Day – the nearest Saturday to the execution date, 17 May.

If that isn't enough to entice you, then consider the words of architect G.E. Street, designer of the Royal Courts of Justice on the Strand in 1870:

'There is, in my opinion, no church in the whole diocese of Oxford which exceeds it in beauty and architectural interest. It is not only that in scale it is grander than most parish churches, but also that in its architectural detail it is singularly rich and beautiful.'

RIGHT: Burford parish church was built in the 1580s and was the scene of a gruesome civil war struggle.

'sheep hills'. The local sheep, affectionately known as the 'Cotswold Lion', was prized for its heavy wool clip, which brought great wealth to Cotswold merchants. Sheep outnumbered people by thousands to one. When the wool industry declined the area paid a heavy price for its dependence on this one source of income. There was little money for further building and development, which goes some way to explaining the unchanged landscape.

The trip continues through the Windrush Valley as far as Minster Lovell. Proceed on to Long Hanborough, which warrants another break. Here, sample a slice of past times with a visit to the Oxford Bus Museum. This commemorates the life of another William Morris, aka Lord Nuffield, who founded the car factory at Cowley in 1912. William Morris utilized Henry Ford's production-line concept and used it to create a low-cost car – the much-loved and massively successful Morris Minor. Lord Nuffield was a great philanthropist and donated around £25 million to advance health care, social education and social welfare.

OXFORD

Oxford is just an 8-mile (12km) ride from Woodstock and on the way one cannot miss the view of the city that inspired Matthew Arnold's words in his poem 'Thyrsis':

Humid the air, leafless, yet soft as spring
The tender purple spray on copse and briars
And that sweet city with her dreaming spires,
She need not June for beauty's heightening.

The actual view comes from a more southerly approach into the city. Nevertheless, the dreamy vision is much the same. Oxford is a city of cyclists; some 20,000 ride the streets daily. Harold Briercliffe observed: 'The distant view of the city from any of the surrounding hills is a most pleasing one, largely because of the grouping of its towers and spires. The residential colleges are famous for their rich halls, chapels and for their green lawns.'

He also urges visitors to see a number of famous buildings, including the Bodleian Library, the main research library of Oxford University, purpose built in 1602 and one of the oldest libraries in Europe; the Sheldonian theatre,

BLENHEIM

When Harold Briercliffe was cycling through the Cotswold heartlands in 1949, only the grounds of Blenheim Palace were open to the public; the house was opened to the paying public just one year later. The historic home of the Churchill family is a masterpiece of English baroque architecture and one of architect John Vanbrugh's most magnificent creations. It was declared a World Heritage Site in 1987. Built to commemorate the Duke of Marlborough John Churchill's victory over the French during the Wars of the Spanish Succession, the Marlboroughs themselves had to find £50,000 to complete it. The house features Grinling Gibbon's intricate carvings, exquisite hand-painted ceilings, tapestries, paintings in almost every room and an extraordinary collection of fine porcelain. Each room is full of breathtaking treasures from the last 300 years.

The fourth Duke of Marlborough brought in Capability Brown to fulfil his vision for the 2,000-acre (809-hectare) park and gardens and in the 1920s the ninth duke employed the French landscape architect Achille Duchêne to redesign the formal gardens, producing the glorious combination of designs we see today. The fabulous water terraces in the grounds are reminiscent of the Parterre d'Eau at Versailles. Winston Churchill was born at Blenheim and proposed to his sweetheart, Clementine Hozier, at the Temple of Diana overlooking the lake.

ABOVE: A bicycle race held at Blenheim Palace fête in August 1947.

designed by Sir Christopher Wren and built between 1664 and 1668 and the St Mary the Virgin parish church. A church has stood on this site since 1280 and was mentioned in the Domesday Book, but the current building, with its ornate spire, dates from 1315. Climb the 124 steps in the tower to enjoy the uninterrupted views of the city. In 1555 the church was the site of the trial of the Oxford Martyrs, in which the Bishops Latimer, Cranmer and Ridley were tried for heresy and subsequently burnt just outside the city walls.

Carfax is considered to be the heart of the city; the name is derived from the French *Carrefour*, meaning crossroads. Carfax Tower is all that remains of the thirteenth-century St Martin's Church, demolished in 1896 so that the road could be widened to accommodate traffic. The Carfax Tower is 74ft (23m) tall and can be climbed for a view of the Oxford skyline. On the east façade the church clock is adorned with two figures that strike the bells every quarter of an hour.

Oxford is preserved in its spectacular entirety unlike the rest of Britain's cities. The fact that it survived the ravages of the Second World War virtually intact is due to Hitler commanding the Luftwaffe to avoid bombing the city. So, then, it is, like the rest of the Cotswolds, apparently steeped in preservative and maintained in mint condition for visitors to enjoy, a glorious historical theatre of days gone by and, for all its artifice, a real pleasure to explore.

ABOVE: Female students cycling in Oxford in 1953, even though women's cycling clothes were still an issue at Oxford in the 1950s. Women were not allowed to wear trousers with academic dress, which was compulsory for lectures.

EASTERN ENGLAND

'As there are no hills or mountains in the fens – the sky always seems much larger and more beautiful'
Charles Kingsley

T he east of England offers miles of beautiful, tranquil beaches and acres of peaceful, undulating countryside stretching as far as the eye can see. If these weren't enough to lure the cyclist then its seductive flatness makes the east even more tantalizing. If you are looking for a corner of the countryside in which to sample cycle touring, want a peaceful holiday with plenty of gentle exercise, or if you have a family – let's be realistic, teenagers are no more enthusiastic about strenuous cycling holidays than toddlers –

then the east cannot be beaten. Even the weather is good – the east coast is one of the driest regions of the UK.

The east incorporates the counties of Essex, Suffolk, Norfolk, and Cambridgeshire. The area is littered with reminders of repeated attack by invaders: Roman remains, Saxon burial grounds, Danish words incorporated into place names and castles aplenty. It was home to many of our most significant historical characters; Boudicca led a tribal uprising against the Romans around AD 60–61, and Hereward the Wake, the eleventh-century Anglo-Saxon who resisted the Norman Conquest, rampaged around the area. Catherine of Aragon, the first of Henry VIII's six wives, died here, and her daughter, Mary Tudor, lived here before she in turn became queen after marshalling her army at Framlingham in Suffolk. Thomas Howard, the calculating and cold-hearted Duke of Norfolk who

LEFT: Wicken Fen, a nature reserve for over 100 years, is one of the most important areas of wetland in Europe. **PAGE 116:** A view of the seaside resort of Great Yarmouth in 1909.

utilized his relatives for personal gain, is buried in St Michael at Framlingham. Mary Boleyn, Henry VIII's mistress, her sister Anne Boleyn, Henry's second wife and Catherine Howard, his fifth wife, all had the misfortune to be Howard's nieces. Thomas Wolsey, later Cardinal Wolsey, was born in Ipswich. Oliver Cromwell came from Huntingdon and Horatio Nelson from Burnham Thorpe in Norfolk.

THE FENS

Great swathes of the eastern landscape, known as the Fens, are only a little above sea level and were once subject to regular seasonal flooding. The area, which lies around the coast of the Wash, has a toe in Lincolnshire, Norfolk, Cambridgeshire and a tiny piece of Suffolk and covers 1,505 square miles (3900 sq km).

The Fens were transformed in the mid-seventeenth century when the Earl of Bedford invited one Cornelius Vermuyden, a Dutch engineer, to try out Dutch reclamation methods: winding rivers were diverted to flow via the most direct route to the sea. Local fishermen and fowlers were hostile towards the land reclamation scheme as it threatened their livelihoods. Oliver Cromwell made representations in parliament on their behalf, for only the king and the engineers stood to profit by the scheme. The area was flooded during the Civil War to prevent Royalist advances, but afterwards the marshland was drained.

Drainage and oxidization causes peat to shrink. The best example of this can be seen at Holme Fen in Lincolnshire where, in 1884, a metal gauge was sunk into the newly drained peat as far as the clay below – its top now stands 13ft (4m) above the surface of the land. It is generally accepted to be the lowest land point below sea level in the UK. Only isolated pockets of true fenland remain, most notably the Ouse Washes where the land is managed traditionally: grazed in summer and flooded in winter.

The drained land was and remains fertile and rich, perfect for growing crops and flowers. Spalding marks the centre of the bulb-growing region – a vision in spring – and flower festivals are a feature of the Fens in the summer months. The drainage process is now in reverse, with many agencies looking to regenerate as much fenland as possible; by working with farmers and commercial growers they aim to minimize the damage caused by fertilisers and effluents and to encourage seasonal flooding.

ABOVE: Painting of Ely town in 1905. The magnificent Norman cathedral, known as the 'Ship of The Fens' dominates the flat fen landscape for miles around.

Wicken Fen is reputed to be one of the most important areas of wetland in Western Europe. A windmill that once pumped water off the land now pumps water on to it; as a result the land is now much higher than the surrounding shrunken peat lands. Insects are particularly abundant, but 29 species of mammal, including otters, water voles and semi-feral konik ponies have been recorded along with more than 200 species of birds.

Ely, the second smallest city in the UK, was once known as The Isle of Eels. It sits in the boggy Fens and remained an island until the surrounding land was drained in the seventeenth and eighteenth centuries. The first religious building on the site was founded by Etheldreda in 673; work on Ely Cathedral, known locally as the 'Ship of the Fens' was begun in 1109. The magnificent Lantern Tower made from wood, lead and glass is considered the jewel in the cathedral's crown. There is plenty of cycling around and about the small city and nearby, in Newmarket – home to the Jockey Club, the controlling body of British horse racing – is the Jockey's Trail. This 28-mile (45km) circular cycle route, heads out across the Fens, crosses chalk grassland and woodland and passes through many small, picturesque villages.

CAMBRIDGE

The city of Cambridge is a cyclist's paradise – just look at the thousands of bicycles whizzing around propelled by cyclists of all shapes and generations. The Romans established a town on the site in AD 70; the first university was set up in 1209 and the first college, Peterhouse, was established in 1284. There are 31 colleges in total today; many were created in the fourteenth and fifteenth centuries and the buildings have been carefully preserved. King's College Chapel was commissioned by Henry VI, who was determined that it would be unequalled in size and beauty. Work was finally completed by Henry VIII – the construction took more than 100 years to complete. The colleges, chapels and

ABOVE: Cycling in Trumpington Street, Cambridge, c. 1950. The scene today would be much the same but the students would be less formally dressed.

gardens are generally open to the public, though there are entrance fees. You can also hire a boat and glide along the River Cam past the Backs, where several colleges back on to the river.

Cycle Route 11 runs from Harlow in Essex up to King's Lynn in Norfolk. Parts of the route are still under development, but eventually it will link Cambridge and Ely.

NORFOLK

The North Norfolk Coast, a designated Area of Outstanding Natural Beauty, stretches over 174 square miles (450 sq km). The coastline swoops in a broad curve between the ports of Great Yarmouth and King's Lynn. There are great sweeps of intertidal sand, salt marsh, mudflats and shingle banks with the shifting sea beyond. The fields beyond the coast are dissected with channels and sand dunes run down to the long deserted beaches. Large chunks of the area are subject to marine erosion and, while the sea is calm in the summer, winter storms can be overwhelming, as illustrated by the devastating floods of 1953.

This is a prime area for birdwatchers and is internationally renowned. Wading birds throng here and migrating birds drop by to feed and rest en route. At the RSPB Reserve at Snettisham, look out for the twice-daily spectacle of thousands of birds flying from the mudflats to avoid the incoming tide. Just inland is Burnham Thorpe, where Nelson was born in 1758.

ABOVE: The Hotchkiss Patent Bicycle Railroad ran on a wooden rail, on a 250ft (76m) diameter circle, at Great Yarmouth between 1895 and 1909 (seen here c. 1900).

Much of the land between Holme-next-the-Sea and Cromer, further around the coast, is remote and dotted with nature reserves. The remains of a Bronze Age timber circle, known as Seahenge, was uncovered at Holme, and removed by English Heritage for preservation. The Peddars Way National Trail,

ABOVE: During one of his cycle rides in Eastern England in the 1950s, Harold Briercliffe took this picture of women at Norwich market enjoying the local cockles.

a 2,000-year-old Roman road, runs for 46 miles (74km) from Holme-next-the-Sea down through countryside to Knettishall Heath in Suffolk. Unusually, most of this national trail for walkers is also open to cyclists.

Some 200 species of birds can be seen at Brancaster and there is a private ferry service to the National Nature Reserve at Scolt Head Island, where an array of terns can be spotted. Boats can also be taken out to the reserve at Blakeney Point – a long sand and shingle spit where you can gaze at seals. Further around the coast is the seaside resort of Great Yarmouth, an inspiration to Dickens and featured in *David Copperfield*.

Inland is the county town of Norwich. The city is home to a splendid cathedral with a Norman nave and tower. Norwich Castle, built in 1067 for William the Conqueror, is perched strategically on a hill. The Marriott's Way

HICKLING
Circular Route
NORFOLK BROADS

DISTANCE: 20 MILES (32KM)   TIME: 3 HOURS

This is a quiet and flat circular route of around 20 miles (32 km) running through a series of picturesque villages in the midst of the beautiful Norfolk Broads. The route should take around 3 hours to cycle, or more if you stop at places along the way.

STARTING PLACES

The suggested starting place is at Hickling Heath. If you are arriving by car there is a public car park adjacent to Hickling Broad. Those arriving by car could also start their circular route at any of the small settlements along the way, such as Horsey or Sea Palling. It is suggested that wherever you start, it would be best to travel anti-clockwise along the route and to allow time to stop at some of the places of interest along the way.

THE ROUTE

At Hickling Heath turn left [1] out of the car park and follow Staithe Road. Turn left [2] and follow Heath Road. Cycle straight on at the Catfield junction [3] and follow signs for Potter Heigham. Turn left along Back Lane [4]. Cross the junction with Decoy Road [5]. Turn left at the junction with Church Lane [6]. Cycle past St Nicholas'

Church and the junction with Marsh Road and continue along Church Lane to the centre of Potter Heigham. You may want to stop here to take a look at the medieval bridge, believed to date from 1385. It is famous for being the most difficult bridge to navigate in the Broads (the bridge opening is so narrow that only small cruisers can pass through it).

Leaving Potter Heigham, you should turn left along Station Road **[7]**. Take great care crossing the busy A149 **[8]** and continue along Station Road, then turn left along Bridge Road **[9]**. Cycle over the bridge then join the cycle track that runs parallel with the Causeway. Take care crossing the mouth of the Causeway at the junction with the A149 **[10]**, then continue to use the cycle track alongside the trunk road until you turn left at Low Road **[11]** and left again at Church Road **[12]**. Follow Church Road and bear left in Repps past the church until you reach the next junction. You will need to take care turning right here **[13]**, then turn almost immediately left to follow Mill Lane to the junction with the A149. Again, you will need to take care as you cross this busy A-road to follow straight on along Repps Road **[14]**.

As you enter Martham turn left along Low Road **[15]** then left again to rejoin Repps Road **[16]**. At the centre of Martham turn left along Black Street **[17]** then bear right in to Staithe Road **[18]**. As you approach West Somerton you should keep to the left when the road forks, then go straight on following the signs for Horsey **[19]**.

Continue to follow the road along a series of sharp bends through Horsey **[20]**. This village is another good place for a stop. You may want to visit the Horsey Mere Nature Reserve and the restored Horsey windpump, which is open daily during the summer months. Continuing on from Horsey, you should head towards Waxham and Sea Palling.

When you reach Sea Palling, cycle past the Beach Road turning on your right (unless you want to stop at the excellent sandy beach) and continue heading out of the village along Stalham Road **[21]**. At the next junction turn left along Hickling Road **[22]**, and then keep following the road as it takes you through Hickling and Hickling Green until you reach the left turn into Stubb Road **[23]**. Follow the road around into Ouse Lane and Staithe Road until you return to the starting point at Hickling Broad.

If you have any energy left after your bike ride you may want to spend some time finding out more about what the beautiful Hickling Broad has to offer. The Broad is one of the largest expanses of open water in East Anglia and is a National Nature Reserve established by English Nature. It is also part of the Upper Thurne Broads and Marshes Site of Special Scientific Interest.

There is a series of other excellent cycle routes in the Norfolk Broads that you may want to try (see Further Information, page 211).

runs for 14 miles (22km) from Norwich, north-west to Reepham along a disused railway track. There are many cycle routes through the area and a number of bicycle-friendly steam-train rides. The Bure Valley Railway, a narrow-gauge steam railway, runs between Aylsham and Wroxham in the heart of the Norfolk Broads and carries bicycles. A 9-mile (14km) cycle track runs alongside the line, so cyclists need only ride one way. The North Norfolk Railway runs between

ABOVE: The Bure Valley Railway is a narrow-gauge steam line, running for 9 miles (14 km) between Aylsham and Wroxham in Norfolk. A cycle path runs alongside the entire length.

Sheringham, Weybourne and Holt, and again it carries bicycles, making it possible to travel in old-fashioned style by an evocative combination of steam train and pedal power.

THE SUFFOLK COAST

Moving south along the crumbling coastline into Suffolk there are the charming resorts of Southwold, Walberswick and Aldeburgh, which maintain an old-fashioned approach to seaside fun with beach huts, a pier, boating lakes and wonderful quantities of fresh fish. The Aldeburgh Music Festival is held every June. Further south, the 88-mile (142km) Suffolk

ABOVE: Suffolk Coastal Route 1 is an undulating 88-mile (140km) circular route set within a designated Area of Outstanding Natural Beauty.

Coastal Cycle Route links the coastal villages between Dunwich and Felixstowe, before returning inland via Framlingham and Woodbridge. At Framlingham you will find a magnificent castle said to have been founded by Raedwald, one of the most powerful kings of the East Angles in the early seventh century. It was the family home of the Earls of Norfolk for centuries but was lost by Thomas Howard, the third Duke of Norfolk, when he was stripped of titles and land by Henry VIII. He was saved from execution by the death of the king; his son, Henry Howard, had the misfortune to be executed just before Henry died. Both are buried in the church at Framlingham.

THE RIVER STOUR

The River Stour runs along the border of Suffolk and Norfolk, marking an unchanged boundary that takes the cyclist across countless old bridges that span the two counties. The area was prosperous in the Middle Ages due to the wool trade and there are many beautiful old houses and villages to be seen. This is Constable country and the landscape that inspired him can be seen all around.

One of John Constable's most famous paintings is *The Haywain*; finished in 1821, it shows Willy Lott's cottage, which has survived virtually unchanged, on the left bank of the Stour with the Essex countryside depicted on the right. The cottage can be seen at Flatford Mill, along with numerous other landscapes painted by the artist, and it is possible to cycle alongside Flatford Lock.

ABOVE: *The Haywain* (1821) by John Constable. Many of Constable's Eastern England landscapes can be cycled, including Flatford Lock.

CYCLE ROUTE

ALTON WATER
Circular Route

SUFFOLK

DISTANCE: 9 MILES (14.5KM)   TIME: 1.5 HOURS

This is a short cycle ride of about 9 miles (14.5km) on mainly traffic-free paths alongside the Alton Water reservoir. The water is home to winter wildfowl and provides summer breeding for great crested grebes and common terns. A range of habitats surrounds the reservoir, including broad-leaved woodland, wild-flower meadows, grassland, reed beds and native scrub.

STARTING PLACE

Alton Water is situated about 4 miles (6km) south of Ipswich, adjacent to the A137 (Ipswich to Manningtree) road. The entrance to the site is on the B1080 in the village of Holbrook, half a mile (0.8km) from the Royal Hospital School. There is a café and cycle-hire outlet at the start point.

THE ROUTE

From the hire shop in Holbrook, you should follow the path around the reservoir in a clockwise direction. Take the track over

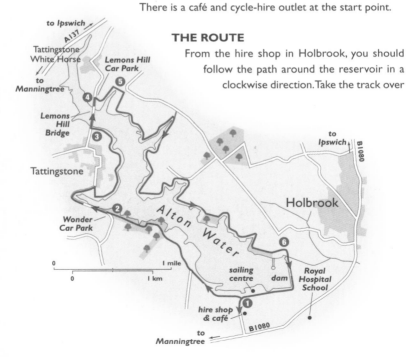

the zebra crossing **[1]** and follow the path for 1½ miles (2.5km) until you reach Wonder Car Park **[2]**.

Take the cycle track through Wonder Car Park and continue for a further 2½ miles (4km) until you reach Lemons Hill Bridge **[3]**, by which time you have almost reached the halfway point.

You should then cycle across the bridge and turn right into Lemons Hill Car Park **[4]** and keep to the grassy track for about ½ a mile (0.8km) until you reach the electric sub-station **[5]**; at this point you have a choice of an alternative minor road route. If you want to keep cycling close to the reservoir you should stay on the original cycle track over the hilly terrain and continue until you reach the dam wall **[6]**. You can then follow the cycle path back past the sailing centre to the start point, just in time for a nice refreshing drink at the café.

ABOVE: Alton Water with its abundant bird life.

NORTHERN ENGLAND

*'Proportion rather than height or width gives the
Lakeland mountains their unique charm'*
Harold Briercliffe

S ome of the finest cycling in the country is to be had in the north of England. There is a range of landscapes to suit all tastes and fitness levels; marvel at the expansive beauty of the North York Moors, gawp at the breathtaking scenery of the Lake District and try pass-storming or test yourself with the swinging ups and downs of the Yorkshire Dales. Follow Hadrian's Wall from west to east and goggle at the spectacular coastal scenery and rugged castles found along the Northumberland coast – a reflection of its turbulent frontier history. Large swathes of the area are densely populated and industrialized and the scars left by dying industries reveal its heritage. The north is also home to some of the country's largest cities: Manchester, Liverpool, Sheffield and Newcastle-upon-Tyne, with good cycle routes and links to the countryside.

South of the cities of Liverpool and Manchester is the Cheshire Plain, which contains rich farmland, wooded ridges and industrial towns such as Macclesfield, where silk was milled, and Nantwich and Northwich, where salt was mined. The City of Chester was built by the Romans to keep the Welsh

ABOVE: A group of 1960s schoolgirls pause to look at the map on a trip out with their teacher in Hatchmere, Cheshire. **PAGE 130:** A view of the Trough of Bowland on the edge of the Bowland Forest in Lancashire.

away from the fertile farmland of the area. Much of the enclosing Roman wall still stands around this pretty medieval city. East of Chester is Delamere Forest, once royal hunting grounds, now Forestry Commission land with 4-mile (6.4km) or 7-mile (11km) cycle routes suitable for families. The Whitegate Way runs from Cuddington, west of Northwich, on a disused railway line and ends at a salt mine a little north of the town of Winsford. Mrs Gaskell married and was buried in Knutsford; she based her novel *Cranford* on the town. A few miles north-east of the town is a 6-mile (10km) ride around Styal Estate and Quarry Bank Mill. The mill is home to the most powerful working waterwheel in Europe and gives visitors a real taste of the life of a mill worker during the Industrial Revolution. South-west from here is the huge radio telescope of Jodrell Bank, surrounded by quiet country lanes; take the train to Goostrey and cycle from there.

THE ISLE OF MAN

The Isle of Man, a self-governing crown dependency situated in the middle of the Irish Sea, has scenic charm, wildlife and old-world character. The Tourist Trophy (TT) races take place every May and June and attract some 50,000 bikers of the motorized type; outside of these months the island is well worth exploring by bicycle. It has 500 miles (800km) of quiet country roads and boasts six designated off-road cycling tracks of varying degrees of difficulty.

LANCASHIRE

The county of Lancashire is shot through with cycle routes: follow National Cycle Route 62 around the Lancashire coast past the extensive sands at Lytham St Anne's and on to the gaudy delights of Blackpool; alternatively, fly through the Lancashire countryside on Route 6 up to the county town of Lancaster. Cycle out to Morecombe, just 3 miles (5km) away,

ABOVE: The Blackpool Tower features in this beer advertisement from 1938.

ABOVE: A cyclist enjoys the peace on a bridleway crossing the moors in north Lancashire near the north Yorkshire border.

on the Lancaster–Morecambe Greenway via the Millennium Bridge; at Morecambe there is a 5-mile (8km) stretch of promenade open to cyclists. Take a walk across the sands, but be careful, the tide is said to come in faster than a galloping horse.

If you are truly ambitious, follow the challenging Lancashire Cycleway on a 280-mile (450km) tour of the county, taking in the wilderness of the Bowland Hills, a designated Area of Outstanding Natural Beauty, the moorland hill country of the south Pennines and the coastal plain. Route 6, an ideal gateway to the Lake District, can also be followed from Lancaster via Arnside and Silverdale on up to Kendal. South of Kendal and just off Route 6 is Sizergh Castle, a stunning medieval house that was extended in Elizabethan times. The interiors are extraordinarily good and the gardens are beautiful too; there are glorious views to be had across Morecambe Bay and up to the Lake District. Also in South Lakeland is Kirkby Lonsdale, where visitors can look from the churchyard over the River Lune Valley. The landscape was described by the nineteenth-century art critic John Ruskin thus: 'I do not know, in all my own country, still less in France or Italy, a place more naturally divine.' Ruskin's View, as it is known locally, was immortalized by J.M.W. Turner. The medieval Devil's Bridge is also close by, but be warned that motorbikers converge on the bridge every Sunday, come rain or shine.

THE LAKE DISTRICT

The scenery of Cumbria's Lake District has inspired poets, artists and writers for centuries and attracts more than 12 million visitors annually. The Lake District National Park is the largest in England. Harold Briercliffe loved the area: '...within this small area is to be found such riches, so little dullness, that it does not suffer in comparison with other and more noted touring regions. In Lakeland everything – or nearly everything – seems to be in accord.' However, he agreed with the notion that the lakes are best seen on foot: 'The tourist who deserts his bicycle to climb hills or to explore valleys or to row will get nearer to the heart of the Lake country than those who cling faithfully to two wheels.'

The key features of the Lake District – its deep U-shaped valleys – were formed by glacial action and meltwater. In the highest peaks glacial cirques (amphitheatre-like valleys) can be seen; these are often filled with tarns – small upland lakes. The topography of the region is likened to a wheel; the hub is just north of Grasmere and the valleys and lakes – the spokes – radiate out from here in a circle. The highest peaks are rocky and bare, while lower down are areas of open moorland and bog. Below the tree line are deciduous woods and conifer plantations, as well as the lakes.

BELOW: Harold Briercliffe admiring the Denthead Railway Viaduct on the Dentdale moors, which graces the highway between Studley Garth and Newby Head.

CYCLE ROUTE

EGREMONT *to* BECKERMET
Circular Route

CUMBRIA

DISTANCE: 15 MILES (24KM)   TIME: 3½ HOURS

This quiet circular route of around 15 miles (24km) follows a series of country lanes between Egremont and Beckermet. It runs parallel to the coast as far as Braystones before turning inland to return to Egremont via Beckermet and Thornhill. The route is hilly in places and should take about 2 to 3 hours to cycle, or more if you stop at places along the way.

STARTING PLACES

There are two suggested places to start. If you are arriving by car there is a car park in the centre of Egremont. Those arriving by train could start the circular route at Nethertown station.

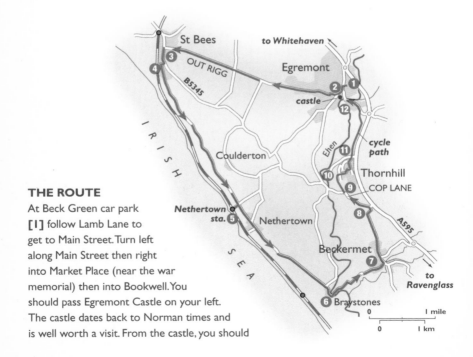

THE ROUTE

At Beck Green car park [1] follow Lamb Lane to get to Main Street. Turn left along Main Street then right into Market Place (near the war memorial) then into Bookwell. You should pass Egremont Castle on your left. The castle dates back to Norman times and is well worth a visit. From the castle, you should take the right-hand fork in the road for St Bees **[2]**. Follow Grove Road, then Baybarrow Road as you leave Egremont and continue on towards St Bees. The road runs directly across higher land through a patchwork of fields before dropping down towards St Bees and the coast.

The approach to St Bees is via Out Rigg, which arrives at the B5345 junction **[3]**. Turn left here and after approximately ½ mile (0.8km) turn right following the sign for Nethertown **[4]**. The road rises again and offers excellent views of the coast, including St Bees Head, the westernmost point of Cumbria, and back inland towards Scafell Pike, the highest mountain in England. It provides a quiet route all the way to Braystones. There are various points along the route where crossroads provide access to the coast (e.g. at Sea Lane). Another right-hand turn provides access down to Nethertown railway station on the Carlisle and Barrow-in-Furness line (this station provides a potential starting point for those who want to use the circular route and arrive by train) **[5]**. Continue straight on at the crossroads until you arrive at Nethertown. The route passes directly south through the village and on to Braystones.

Arriving at the edge of Braystones, continue along the road into the village and pass Beck Close on your right, then bear left following the sign for Beckermet. **[6]**. The hedge-lined road between the two villages is narrow and includes a series of hairpin bends. It will not take long to reach Beckermet. Continue along Braystones Road to the centre of Beckermet until you reach the junction with Morass Road **[7]**. Turn left here and head north out of the village towards Thornhill. Continue to follow Morass Road for about 1 mile (1.6km), then turn left when you reach Cop Lane **[8]**. When you reach a sharp left turn in the road, you will notice a cycle path that continues straight ahead **[9]** and which provides a traffic-free link to Thornhill.

Thornhill is a settlement with a much more recent history than the other villages along the route. It was created in the 1920s as part of the national campaign to improve housing conditions, keeping a promise made by the government to veterans of the First World War. When you reach the end of the cycle path, follow the cut through and turn left along Wodow Road **[10]**. Then turn right along Kersey Road, left at Ehen Road, left again at the Knoll and finally right at Thorny Road. This takes you to the corner of Dent Road with High Road, which is where the A595 cycle track starts **[11]**. The cycle track runs parallel with the A595 and provides an excellent traffic-free link back to Egremont. The route back to the Beck Green car park is via Vale View. Then turn right into South Street [12] then right again into Main Street before arriving at Lamb Lane and the car park.

ABOVE: Motorists and cyclists stop to admire the view of Grasmere from the top of Dunmail Raise, the reputed site of the burial mound of Dunmail, the last king of Cumbria.

The area is known to be the wettest part of England; average annual rainfall is more than 6ft 6in (2m): cyclists be warned! The driest months of the year are March to June, the wettest are October through to January. Most cyclists would be advised to avoid the area in winter, when the weather can be quite brutal.

The Lake District has been inhabited for more than 10,000 years and contains 6,000 archaeological sites, including 200 scheduled ancient monuments. There are a number of stone circles built during the Neolithic and Bronze Ages, and newly discovered examples of prehistoric rock art.

There are more than 14 lakes and tarns in the Lake District. Strictly speaking, there is only one 'lake', Bassenthwaite Lake, in the district; all the others are called meres or waters – as in Grasmere, Windermere, Coniston Water and Derwent Water. There is wonderful cycling to be had around many of the 'lakes' and there is a Cross Lakes shuttle, ferry and bus, which can take the strain. This can also take you up to Hill Top, Beatrix Potter's house, but there are plenty of pretty cycle routes nearby if your legs can manage the uphill sections. The bus has cycle-carrying facilities between Bowness and Grizedale. Donald Campbell smashed the world speed record on Coniston Water, dying

MOUNTAIN BIKING
IN GRIZEDALE FOREST

Grizedale Forest is the largest in the Lake District, situated between Coniston Water and Windermere. It was decimated in the eighteenth century and left virtually empty. The Forestry Commission has restored oak, spruce, larch and pine woodland. There are five way-marked trails of varying levels in the forest and a new North Face Trail designed to suit adrenaline junkies. There are beautiful lakeside tracks around Brotherswater from which you can see Dove Crag, one of the steepest crags in the Lake District. At Ullswater, there is a route for mountain bikers.

ABOVE: Mountain bikers enjoy the 'rough stuff' in the magnificent Grisedale Forest, which has a challenging, leg-burning and adrenaline-pumping route as well as some gentler family trails.

PASS-STORMING

Pass-storming became *de rigueur* for enthusiastic cyclists in the 1930s and 1940s, long before the advent of mountain bikes and advanced gear systems. And it all started in the Lake District. The concept was simple: you rode your bicycle where you could and when you couldn't you carried it on your back and walked – or ran. The earliest record attempt dates back to 1890, when one Amos Sugden reported that he had taken his bicycle, weighing 50lb (22kg), over Sty Head Pass in the heart of the Lake District. In essence it was an early form of mountain biking, a refusal to accept that when the road ended the cyclist could not continue and cross all terrain, and was also referred to as 'rough stuff'. As bicycles have improved and their design has become more action-specific, the differences between pass-stormers and mountain bikers has become wider again. Mountain bikers want to ride the whole time and will avoid routes that do not allow them to do this. Pass-stormers regard walking as part of the experience and the challenge for them is crossing some of the most difficult mountain passes. Caution must be exercised, however, as with hill walking; cyclists need to be properly equipped with an Ordnance Survey map, a watch, a compass, food, proper protective clothing and footwear and a mobile phone. Pass-storming should not be undertaken solo, but with a partner in case problems arise.

ABOVE: The perverse pleasure of pass-storming.

Harold Briercliffe was an enthusiastic pass-stormer:

'By using footpaths instead of roads, the true lover of the country gets right away from the noise of the main roads and into the heart of the mountain country. His lightweight bicycle is not a great hindrance, certainly not much more so than the immense rucksacks that some of the walking fraternity adopt.'

He relished the exciting cycling that narrow footpaths provided and found it allowed him to undertake interesting circular rides.

during an attempt in 1967 when his boat flipped over at 320mph (515kph). The boat, *Bluebird*, was not found until 2001. Have a break from cycling and take a gondola across Coniston Water to see Brantwood, Ruskin's stunning house. From Coniston you can cycle up to Tarn Hows for the wonderful views; the landscape was in part artificially created in the nineteenth century when three tarns were joined together, and it has become a popular beauty spot.

The Lakeland fells are breathtakingly lovely throughout the year and despite the volume of tourists they still feel wild and remote. Scafell Pike was given to the National Trust in memory of the local men who fell in the First World War. Wasdale is a deep, steep, inaccessible and unspoilt valley with Wast Water at its floor. The wooded ravine at Aira Force goes through beautiful scenery and leads to the High Force waterfalls. A number of cycle routes pass close by; a challenging route is to go over the Kirkstone Pass from Kirkstone to Ambleside. This is a distance of about 3 miles (5km), but the gradient is a climb of between 1:5 and 1:4. There are two choices of descent routes – one, to Troutbeck, is gentler on the brakes.

ABOVE: Wast Water is the deepest piece of water in the Lake District at 258ft (79m). It sits at the bottom of the Wast Water Valley, at the head of which are some of the highest mountains in England.

This is fabulous cycling countryside and there are several long trails with plenty of ascents to test the legs. The Cumbria Way Cycle Route is a 72-mile (115km) route that runs from Ulverston to Carlisle via Keswick, with optional off-road sections. Don't confuse it with the Cumbria Way, a parallel route for hikers. Different again is the Cumbria Cycle Way, a 260-mile (418km) circular on-road route that loosely follows the Cumbrian borders.

Hadrian's Cycleway is a 174-mile (280km) coast-to-coast ride along the length of Hadrian's Wall, a World Heritage site. The wall was built to separate the Romans from the 'barbarians' of the north and marked the frontier of the Roman Empire in Britain for 300 years. It took Hadrian's army four years to build the 73-mile (117km) barrier and it was completed in AD 126. Forts and mile castles were dotted along the length and manned by an army of 10,000 men. The route starts in Ravenglass on the Cumbrian coast and crosses over to Tynemouth in Northumberland on the eastern coast. It can be cycled east to west but is an easier journey tackled west to east, as this takes advantage of the short, steep hills followed by long downhill runs.

On the east coast, the Coast & Castles Route runs from Edinburgh right down to Newcastle and allows you to see some of the finest sights on the Northumberland coast. It covers about 200 miles (322km), 39 (63km) of which are off road, and is generally travelled south to north, this giving some advantage in terms of wind direction.

THE FARNE ISLANDS AND LINDISFARNE

The Farne Islands and Lindisfarne, otherwise known as Holy Island, are situated off the north Northumberland coast and should not be overlooked when cycling in the area. There are 28 Farne Islands in total, many off limits and famous for nesting seabirds, including puffins, guillemot, eider duck and a colony of grey seals.

Lindisfarne, a tiny tidal island north of the Farnes, is closest to the mainland coast; a causeway provides a twice-daily link as the tide retreats, making it a most memorable cycle ride. The remains of the seventh-century priory, dissolved by Henry VIII, can be seen as well as the extraordinary sixteenth-century castle, refurbished by Edward Lutyens, which perches on top of Beblowe Crag. It can be reached on bicycle via the 3-mile (5km) long causeway, but great care must be taken to check tide times on the causeway notice board.

ABOVE: The remains of the sixteenth-century castle perched atop Beblowe Crag on Lindisfarne. The site, accessible by bicycle, has treats for those looking for history as well as stunning wildlife.

Cycling south through the windswept scenery one finds the breathtaking coastal castle of Bamburgh. It was established in AD 547 by King Ida the Flamebearer, who conquered Northumberland; however, the castle we see today took shape in Norman times. Further south again is the ancient fortified village of Warkworth.

Cycle Route 1, which runs all the way from Dover right up to the Shetlands via John o' Groats, runs along the County Durham coastline from Stockton up to Sunderland. Another option is to cross over the county on the 234-mile (376km) Sea-to-Sea Route, a challenging ride that takes you across the Consett-Sunderland railway path (26 miles/42km of disused railway path), to Black Hill, the most northerly of three gritstone plateaux that dominate the Dark Peak region – a miserable place when the weather is bad – over the Pennines into the northern Lake District. The advice is to ride west to east, given the direction of the prevailing winds.

NORTH YORK MOORS

The North York Moors are famous for huge expanses of open heather moor, the largest in England and Wales, steep-sided dales and a 26 mile (42km) section of dramatic North Sea coastline fringed with towering cliffs. The area is situated to the north and east of the city of York and covers an area of 554 square miles (1436 sq km); approximately one third of this total comprises moorland.

The moorland plateau is cut by river valleys. Some are wide and grassy and criss-crossed with dry-stone walls and are used for grazing sheep and cattle. Woodland covers around 22 per cent of the National Park and there are both forestry plantations and mixed deciduous woodland. The White Rose Cycle Route from Hull to Middlesbrough runs across the moors. At the market town of Helmsley you should see the ruins of Helmsley Castle and nearby the ruins of Rievaulx Abbey and Byland Abbey.

ABOVE: The Moor to Sea cycle route links Scarborough, Pickering and Whitby. Here, a view of Fryup Dale from above Danby.

At the Bridestones and Crosscliff Estate, the famous giant weathered Jurassic sandstone outcrops can be seen and there is ancient woodland said to date from the last Ice Age. At the northern end of Crosscliff Moor is Blakey Topping, which commands impressive views across the moor. The Moor to Sea Cycle Route covers 80 miles (129km) of forest tracks, lanes and the former coastal railway and links the towns of Scarborough, Pickering and Whitby.

The Esk Valley Railway 21-mile (35km) cycle route follows the River Esk from its source high on the moors to the coastal town of Whitby, famed for its black jet. The ruins of St Hilda's Abbey sit on the east cliffs of Whitby, as does the parish church of St Mary, whose graveyard gave Bram Stoker the inspiration for *Dracula*. Robin Hood's Bay, whose narrow streets plunge down to the sea, was a favourite haunt of Harold Briercliffe, who recommended it as a base for touring the area on short excursions, such as to Beggar's Bridge and Goathland.

ABOVE: Lewis Carroll is said to have been inspired to write *The Walrus and the Carpenter* during walks on Whitby Sands. It is edged with brightly coloured beach huts that take a regular battering from winter storms.

THE YORKSHIRE DALES

It is perhaps the contrasts of the Yorkshire Dales – the swerving ups and downs – that make it such a charming landscape. The high, wide, open and remote fells are dissected by deep valleys, or dales, lush with woodland and gentle farmland. Most of the area is part of the Yorkshire Dales National Park – the third largest National Park in the UK, covering 683 square miles (1769 sq km). The bulk of the Dales is in Yorkshire, though in the north-west it has a toe in Cumbria. They lie between the Lake District in the west and the North York Moors in the east and straddle the Pennines. Harold Briercliffe believed that 'the Yorkshire Dales yield some of the best cycling in Britain. There are nearly always two roads up each valley…while almost every valley head has an outlet head into the neighbouring dales.'

The Yorkshire Dales are made up of sedimentary rocks of limestone and sandstone, topped with millstone grit, all subject to lifting, folding and glacial action over the millennia. The underlying rock in the area is principally carboniferous limestone, which produces such scenic features as cliffs, crags, scars and limestone pavements. Limestone pavements can be seen at Malham Cove and Ingleborough Nature Reserve. Gaping Gill on the slopes of Ingleborough peak is the largest limestone cave in Britain; also visit the nearby Ingleborough Cave.

KILBURN *and* BYLAND ABBEY
Circular Route

NORTH YORKSHIRE

DISTANCE: 12 MILES (19KM)   TIME: 2 HOURS

This circular route passes through a series of picturesque villages and some dramatic scenery. Before you leave Kilburn, or after your ride, you may want to call in at the Visitors' Centre. This celebrates the work of the 'mouse man' – wood carver Robert Thompson, born in 1876. He is famous for his carvings that are found in many churches and which have his signature mouse hidden somewhere on them. The 12-mile (19km) route should take around 2 hours to cycle, or more if you stop at places along the way.

This route uses parts of the National Byway, a series of signposted leisure cycle routes around Britain, some 4,500 miles (7,242km) in total. It uses some of the most attractive and traffic-light existing country lanes and, as in this example, it provides opportunities to visit several places of historic interest.

STARTING PLACES

There are two suggested places to start the circular route if arriving by car. There is some parking in Kilburn near the War Memorial. Alternatively, there is a car park at Byland Abbey. Wherever you start, it is suggested that you cycle the loop in an anti-clockwise direction.

Those wanting to tackle a longer route in the area could try the National Byway 25-mile (40km) loop starting at Easingwold.

THE ROUTE

If starting in Kilburn **[1]**, head south, following the road signs for Coxwold. Cycle straight on as you pass the left turn for High Kilburn and head out of the village. Continuing south along Whinny Bank you will cycle through pleasant agricultural land with views back towards the hills where you can see the famous Kilburn White Horse. This White Horse dates from 1857 and is the largest such hillside figure in the UK. It was created by schoolmaster John Hodgson and his pupils who helped mark the horse and cut away the topsoil to reveal the underlying rock and exposed scree (which was then whitewashed). The horse has survived a difficult history. A severe hailstorm caused significant damage in the 1890s and the horse outline fell into disrepair after the First World War. A campaign by the *Yorkshire Evening Post* led to the horse being repaired in 1925. The outbreak of the Second World War meant that it had to be covered and hidden from view until 1946, when it was uncovered and whitened. In the postwar years, a series of storms threatened the White Horse once again until a restoration fund was established. Today, the White Horse Association looks after the horse in partnership with local farmers.

Its large size means that the White Horse is visible from many miles but the view gradually diminishes as you cycle south. You will reach a T-junction where you should turn right **[2]**. Cycle into Coxwold, passing the picturesque St Michael's Church. When you reach the centre of the village take the left turn for Byland Abbey **[3]**. You will have a good view of the impressive abbey ruins as you approach from the south; it is well worth spending some time here. This abbey dates from around 1177; upon its completion in the late twelfth century it was said to be the largest and most elaborate Cistercian building in Europe and by the sixteenth century the abbey had become a very prosperous place. But it was surrendered to Henry VIII on 30 November 1538 and fell victim to the pillaging and destruction of the Dissolution of the Monasteries, resulting in the abbey's gradual and terminal decline.

As you leave Byland Abbey, turn left **[4]** and follow the signs for Oldstead. You will now pass through some dramatic scenery with Elm Hag Lake and Woods to your right (rising to Snever Scar beyond) and Brink Hill on your left. Follow the road round to the right as you reach Oldstead **[5]**. Bear to the left **[6]** and cycle alongside Scawling Wood, following Oldstead Road until turning left along River Road towards High Kilburn **[7]**. River Road is rather hilly through High Kilburn. You will then reach another T-junction where you should turn right **[8]** into Kilburn before making your way back to your starting point.

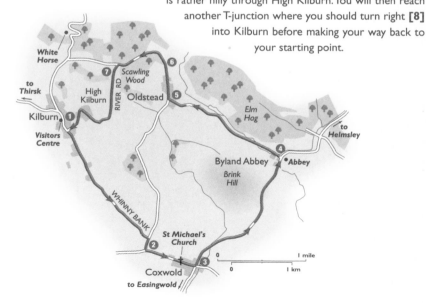

The larger southern dales run almost parallel north to south and are less remote, while to the north the dales run from west to east. Most take their name from the rivers that run through them – Swaledale, for example, is cut through by the River Swale.

Water pours down from the Pennines and vanishes into swallow holes in the chalk; caves and gorges further fracture the limestone. White Scar Cave, the longest show cave in the UK, was formed under one of the Three Peaks – Ingleborough – and is pocked with stalactites and stalagmites. The Settle Loop of the Pennine Bridleway is a 10-mile (16km) circuit that takes in some of the stunning Three Peaks scenery.

Bolton Castle is a spectacular medieval fortress in the heart of Wensleydale. Mary Queen of Scots was imprisoned here and it was besieged during the Civil War in 1645. A section of the Yorkshire Dales Cycleway takes visitors through this part of the country.

The area has been inhabited for centuries and as a result moorland accounts for half of the Dales. Marsden Moor covers around 5,685 acres (2,300 hectares) of unenclosed common moorland with peaks, crags, a reservoir and valleys. Birds such as golden plover, red grouse, curlew and twite can be seen through the heather and cotton grass. The moor was the site of a terrible battle between Royalist and Parliamentary armies in the English Civil War on 2 July 1644; the Royalists suffered a massive defeat. The Pennine Bridleway, suitable for mountain bikers, runs along the west side of Marsden Moor and on to the south Pennines.

There are many wonderful cycle routes dissecting the dales. The circular 130-mile (210km) Yorkshire Dales Cycle Way has plenty to challenge the cyclist; however, the whole area does not have to be tackled. The route starts in Skipton, known as the 'gateway to the Dales', climbs over moorland to Wharfdale, takes you past Settle and near to the Ingleborough Show Cave and the Waterfalls Walk at Ingleton. Move through five of the Yorkshire Dales – Kingsdale, Deepdale,

ABOVE: A peaceful route through Widdop Moor, an exquisite landscape with just sheep for company.

ABOVE: A 1929 illustration of Petergate, which stands in the shadows of York Minster. Guy Fawkes lived in this street long before he hatched the infamous gunpowder plot.

Dentdale, Widdale and Wensleydale – then continue over Askrigg Common and drop into Swaledale. The final leg returns you to Skipton via Wharfdale and Bolton Abbey. Families or sedate tourers can focus on the valley bottoms, while the muscle-crunching enthusiast can tackle the hefty peaks. But, as Harold Briercliffe observed, this is a perfect area for touring – you can base yourself in one spot and sample any number of different routes as demanding or heritage-filled as you like. While you are in the area, remember that this is Brontë country and take a visit out to the Brontë Parsonage Museum to see the home and the surrounding countryside that so inspired the three sisters.

The Pennine Bridleway enters the Yorkshire Dales National Park at Long Preston and meanders through 52 miles (84km) of countryside via Settle, Malham Moor, Feizor, Austwick, Selside and Newby Head. It moves out of the National Park at the Cumbria boundary above Garsdale.

Don't overlook the medieval city of York on your travels. York Minster, the largest gothic cathedral north of the Alps, with some of the finest stained-glass windows in the world, is simply breathtaking. Harold Briercliffe describes it as the handiest of all starting places for a tour of the Yorkshire Moors and coast and 'one of the most fascinating towns in the whole of England'.

BRACING VENTILATION IN YORKSHIRE

'They call this Brontë country. But cycling author Harold Briercliffe came here for reasons that had nothing to do with literature. For him the celebrated sisters of Haworth Parsonage came a poor second to the area's majestic countryside. Its deep ravines, clear running streams and wild uplands – they were the real attraction.'

CLARE BALDING

The desolate Yorkshire moors have a spirit and character all their own, yet the evocative tales of the Brontë sisters, who lived in Haworth, render the landscape strangely familiar. It is a challenging environment: its history serves as a reminder that living amid such dramatic, untamed beauty is not without its hardships.

Our journey begins in Hebden Bridge, West Yorkshire. Harold Briercliffe, not usually lost for words, had little to say about the town – perhaps his silence was in itself revealing. He visited in the late 1940s when the once-prosperous mill town was in decline – the textile industry on which its fortunes were based was experiencing a serious downturn.

Hebden Bridge developed as a useful crossing point of the River Hebden – the packhorse bridge dates back to 1510. There is a steep hill into and out of the market town and it is these very gradients, the cycling highs and lows, as well as the town's proximity to wool markets, that made it an ideal centre for water-powered weaving mills in the eighteenth century, specializing in the production of corduroy and worsted. A local entrepreneur recognized that the town should manufacture clothing as well as cloth, and it developed into an important area for the manufacture of workers' clothing. As the industry died, the town reinvented itself and became a tourist centre for the area, in part due to its proximity to the Pennine Way and local beauty spot Hardcastle Crags.

ABOVE: Clare Balding takes a breath of bracing Yorkshire air at the start of her 30-mile (48km) tour of the Calder Valley.

YORKSHIRE

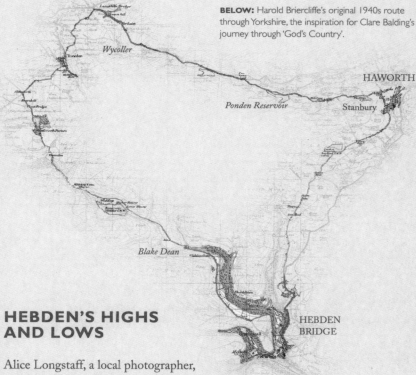

BELOW: Harold Briercliffe's original 1940s route through Yorkshire, the inspiration for Clare Balding's journey through 'God's Country'.

Wycoller

HAWORTH

Ponden Reservoir

Stanbury

Blake Dean

HEBDEN
BRIDGE

HEBDEN'S HIGHS AND LOWS

Alice Longstaff, a local photographer, monitored the changing face of the town over her lifetime. She was apprenticed to a photographic studio, Crossley Waterman, in 1921 at just 13 years of age and took over the business 15 years later in 1936. She worked as a photographer in Hebden Bridge for more than 70 years, creating a unique photographic record of the local community and only stopping, because of ill-health, nine months before her death in 1992. In purchasing the business she acquired old files of images dating back to the 1890s so the total collection, which spans almost a century, contains some 10,000 photographs. Although her images inevitably highlight dramatic changes, they also show a surprising continuity in the town she loved; while

ABOVE: An evocative picture of 'Top Withens' in 1958. Emily Brontë used this house as inspiration for the fictional Wuthering Heights.

shops, cafés, and businesses come and go, the integral heart of the town changes but a little.

Leaving Hebden Bridge, the route climbs out of the Calder Valley where, towards the top, there is a wonderful view of the wooded vale off Hardcastle Crags. This has been a tourist attraction since Victorian days, when workers would catch a train to Hebden and escape into the nearby countryside on their one day off each week. The valley is now owned by the National Trust and is home to 400 acres (160 hectares) of unspoilt woodland, criss-crossed by tumbling streams and waterfalls and mighty millstone-grit stacks. Briercliffe describes them as certainly deserving a visit, and notes: 'The river scenery is of a very high order, the brown pebbly brook and the abundant trees making a delightful picture at any time of year,' though he does sound a note of caution. 'Weekends in summer, however, should not be spent at Hardcastle Crags, as the valley is something of a trippers' haunt.'

Take a trip to Haworth and then go on west, through the old village of Stanbury. Briercliffe reports that this marks the return to wild upland: 'it is more in keeping with the wild spirit of *Wuthering Heights* than modern Haworth.' Nearby is what Harold describes as the 'so-called Brontë waterfall on the Sladen Beck', a feature he berates as 'hardly worth a visit because of itself alone'. Charlotte Brontë was rather more enamoured; she recorded her first visit, after snowfall, in her diary of 29 November 1854: 'It was fine indeed; a perfect torrent racing over the rocks, white and beautiful!' Top Withens, the decayed ruin of a farmhouse said to be the inspiration for the building Wuthering

RIGHT: The painting *Heathcliff Returns* (1993) by Jonathan Barry presents another view of the magnificent moorland of Wuthering Heights.

HAWORTH

In just one year, 1847, each of the Brontë sisters living at Haworth produced a novel; Charlotte wrote *Jane Eyre*, Emily wrote *Wuthering Heights* and Anne wrote *Agnes Grey*, all of which were popular successes. Harold was clearly not a devotee, however, and wrote bruisingly: 'The writings of three sisters, daughters of an incumbent of Irish extraction with a French name, together with the human weaknesses of their brother, have brought to this hilly Yorkshire townlet a fame that has spread — with the usual results — to the far corners of Hollywood.'

The sisters' home, a parsonage, has been turned into a museum offering a fascinating insight into the smallest details of their lives. Much of the planning and writing was undertaken in the dining room and every night the girls would walk around the table until 11pm, reading and discussing their ideas. After Emily and Anne died, a servant reported that Charlotte walked on in solitude, unable to sleep without this nightly ritual. Charlotte did not tell her father that she had written a book until she presented him with a copy of it in his study. Patrick Brontë announced, 'Children, Charlotte has been writing a book and I think it is a better one than I had expected.'

RIGHT: A metal sign for The Bronte Parsonage Museum at Haworth.

Heights, is situated 1½ miles (2km) from Stanbury in the midst of magnificent moorland. Also on the route, close to the Ponden reservoir, is Ponden Hall, which provided the inspiration for the Lintons' home, Thrushcross Grange, in *Wuthering Heights*.

Over the border into Lancashire, Briercliffe's home county, is the hamlet of Wycoller, whose origins can be traced back to 1000 BC. Like many villages in the area its fortune was linked to wool, and it was a thriving farming and weaving community in the sixteenth century. The coming of powered looms led to its decline and 100 years ago it was all but abandoned. Today there are many ruins and a handful of carefully preserved homes. The picturesque hamlet has been declared a conservation area and 350 acres (142 hectares) of surrounding farmland made into a country park.

The remains of Wycoller Hall – reputed to be the inspiration for Ferndean Manor in *Jane Eyre*, the building to which Mr Rochester retires after being maimed and blinded – are found in the hamlet. A special feature of the hall is the great fireplace, which Charlotte describes so vividly in the final chapter of her novel, where Mr Rochester rests his head in despair as Jane, finally returned to him, watches in silence. Wycoller Hall has been empty for many years; its last owner, Squire Henry Cunliffe, died in 1818 leaving substantial debts. The building fell into disrepair and its stonework was used for other local buildings.

THE RUINS OF WYCOLLER

It was around the time of Harold's visit in 1948 that the Friends of Wycoller was founded to help conserve the historic house and village. The campaign was driven by a local librarian, one Evelyn Jowett, who had noted that the ruins were deteriorating year by year. Local volunteers worked on fundraising and by 1951 invasive trees had been removed along with

LEFT: The ruins of Wycoller Hall. This building provided the inspiration for Ferndean Manor in Charlotte Brontë's *Jane Eyre*.

ABOVE: Clare shelters from the rain with historian John Bentley inside a huge fireplace at Wycoller Hall.

rubble and debris, and restoration works undertaken to preserve the hall and improve amenities in the village. The group continued work until 1963; without their efforts Wycoller Hall would undoubtedly have been lost. It is now preserved and protected by a conservation order.

While the Brontë sisters may have left Harold cold, the bridges of Wycoller evoke rather more passion:

> 'A clear stream flows down the dell to enter the village close to a 13th-century pack-horse bridge of double arches. There is another bridge too, consisting of three large slabs on boulders, akin to the clapper bridge at Tarr Steps, in Somerset; while not far away a single-slab bridge recalls the bridges of Dartmoor.'

Seven bridges cross the beck in total; the three to which Briercliffe refers are the most important. The Pack Horse Bridge is thought to be around 800 years old, while the Clam Bridge, the single gritstone slab, may be more than 1,000 years old and is listed as an ancient monument. It was swept away in 1989 and 1990 but was repaired and put back in place. The Clapper Bridge dates from the late eighteenth or early nineteenth century. Grooves were made in the bridge by the clogs of hundreds of weavers who crossed it regularly; they were repeatedly chiselled flat by a farmer whose only daughter was fatally injured after tripping on the bridge.

The hamlet, which has flooded on many occasions, was almost lost in the 1890s when plans were developed to build a reservoir by damming Wycoller Beck in order to meet the increasing demands for water from the nearby town of Colne. The proposals were put on hold for many years but the threat remained strong until Lancashire County Council purchased the land from the Water Board in 1973. It is not clear from Harold's guides whether he was ever aware of such debates in the course of his travels, or realized that some of his beloved beauty spots were close to being lost, but perhaps in lauding their value, he helped ensure their future.

THE INTERNATIONAL ORDER OF THE HENPECKED CLUB

From Wycoller the journey continues up over the moors and back into Yorkshire through Blake Dean, the upper part of Hardcastle Crags. On a hairpin bend on the descent, there was once a chapel where the Society of Henpecked Husbands used to meet. The International Order of the Henpecked Club was founded in 1904 by six preachers. Meetings were shrouded in mystery in case sharp-tongued wives rumbled them. The only prerequisite of membership was that men had to be truly 'under the thumb'. There was a strict men-only rule, though this appears to have been waived in 1974, the club's final year, as minutes show one honorary female member.

Where Wycoller escaped being submerged by a reservoir, Walshaw Dean was not so fortunate. Expanding centres of industry and the growth of large cities increased demand for water, and the steep-sided Pennine valleys were ideal reservoir locations. In 1900 a team of Irish navvies was recruited to build three reservoirs. They moved into the area with their families and a wooden-hutted encampment evolved; it was dubbed 'Dawson City' after the city that sprang up in the wake of the Klondike Gold Rush. A trestle bridge was constructed to carry men and materials from the shanty town to the reservoir. It stood 105ft (32m) tall and ran for 700ft (213m); you will not be surprised to learn that it swayed alarmingly in the wind. The reservoirs were officially opened in 1908 and Dawson City became a ghost town.

SYLVIA PLATH

'Thereafter, as the valley of Hebden Water deepens on the left and becomes Hardcastle Crags, the road hangs above it in an aerial fashion, giving revealing glimpses of the dark woods that hang below' observed Briercliffe. Ten years after Harold passed through, a then little-known poet called Sylvia Plath lived in the area for a short time with her husband and fellow poet Ted Hughes. Like the Brontë sisters she drew inspiration from the landscape:

ABOVE: Sylvia Plath's grave at Heptonstall has been repeatedly vandalised: the inscription from Ted Hughes has been chiselled away by her fans.

> *'Granite ruffs, their shadows*
> *The guise of leaves. The whole landscape*
> *loomed absolute'*
> from 'Hardcastle Crags', Sylvia Plath

Dogged by depression throughout her life, Plath tragically committed suicide just a few years later and was buried in St Thomas' Church in nearby Heptonstall. The village, reputed to be the oldest in Yorkshire, has narrow cobbled streets. The road out of Heptonstall swings high above Hebden Water for the rest of the journey before diving, at an alarming gradient, down back into Hebden Bridge once again.

The high moors and lowland valleys of South-west Yorkshire have given so much to those who have lived on it, worked on it and been inspired by it. But as much as men have played a strong part in carving out this landscape – from the mills to the reservoirs – women have played a unique role in preserving its landscape and celebrating the lives of local people.

WALES

'Classic North Wales has been explored by cyclists since touring on two wheels began. One coastal, several moorland and three main valley routes are open to the Saxon coming in from the east.' Harold Briercliffe

Cyclists will find some of the most beautiful scenery in the country in Wales. Aside from the rugged mountain peaks of Snowdonia in Gwynedd and Clwyd and the desolate heights of the Brecon Beacons in northern Dyfed and southern Powys, there is mile upon mile of stunning coastal scenery in Pembrokeshire and in the Gower Peninsula. Explore the varied landscape of the Marches, which follow the borders of England and Wales (see chapter 5 on Central England). Wales is also blessed with some excellent cycle routes, both short and long distance, which enable you to explore the countryside in peace and safety. The landscape is dotted with magnificent castles, glorious churches and a wealth of interesting flora and fauna. Great swathes have remained unchanged for hundreds of years and are interwoven with myth and legend. 'No touring area in Britain can show so many earthworks, castles or as many bridges notable for their antiquity, legends, beauty or engineering,' observes the normally critical Harold Briercliffe.

The whole area is a magnet for mountain bikers, but a joy for tourers as well. The Clwydian Range, in Clwyd just over the border of north-east Wales, is often overlooked. It has magnificent scenery, is blissfully quiet and has hundreds of miles of well-publicized cycle tracks for all abilities. The Forestry Commission has opened numerous trails to cyclists throughout Wales; some are only suitable for mountain bikes, but many are good for families, too; check the options within your area of choice.

ABOVE: A 1940s cyclist stops for a breather between Beddgelert and Porthmadoc to admire the rugged Aberglaslyn Pass.

The North Wales Coastal Pathway runs along the coast between Talacre and Penmaenmawr for 34 miles (55km). Cycle along the seafronts of Prestatyn, Rhyl, Kinmel Bay, Pensarn, Llandulas, Colwyn Bay, Rhos-on-Sea, Penrhyn Bay, Deganwy, and Conwy, where the medieval fortress of Conwy Castle looms large. It also passes through Llandudno, but an ancient by-law prevents cycle riding along the seafront. Further along the coast, past medieval Caernarvon Castle, is the Llyn Peninsula, where the hills drop to the sea. The area is dissected by some very pretty, quiet country lanes and has 47 miles (76km) of coastline to explore.

SNOWDONIA

Snowdonia in north Wales is home to an immense National Park, which covers some 838 square miles (2,170 sq km). The park extends far beyond the mountainous region around Snowdon, Wales's tallest mountain, pushing south of the medieval town of Conwy on the north Wales coast, to Caernarfon in the west, south to Aberdyfi and east to Lake Bala, the largest freshwater lake in Wales. The scenery is breathtaking; there are soaring mountain peaks, dramatic sweeping valleys, rocky cliffs and sheltered sandy beaches. The area offers some of the most brutal, exhilarating and challenging cycling in the country.

The northernmost mountainous area is the most visited and includes the mountain ranges of Moel Hebog, which contains Mynydd Mawr and the Nantile Ridge, the Snowdon massif and the steep cliffs of the Glyderau. Snowdon itself is so busy that an agreement has been reached between cycling organizations and local councils restricting cyclists' access to the bridleways that lead to the summit of Snowdon. Access is restricted from May to September

BELOW: A cyclists pedals through Nant Gwynant with the glistening waters of Llyn Gwynant behind her. Harold Briercliffe described Nant Gwynant as 'the richest of all the mountain valleys of Snowdonia'.
PAGE 158: Touring cyclists in the 1930s at the summit of Bwlchgroes in mid-Wales.

ABOVE: Two 1950s cyclists contemplate stopping for tea near the clear waters of Tal-y-Llyn, which sits in the shadow of Cadair Idris.

and to the hours between 10.00am and 5.00pm. It is in all our interests that the delicate balance between the protection of the landscape and promoting public access is maintained. So pick your time, go by foot, or have a day off and take the train to the summit. The Snowdon region has one of the wettest climates in the UK, so pack good waterproofs.

Harold Briercliffe is lyrical about the area, maintaining it has the grandest road passes, the most gracious valleys, the shapeliest hills, the most romantic passes and so on. While he acknowledges that, even in his time, it was busy, he also concludes that 'Snowdonia deserves to be visited, and visited early, in the lifetime of every cyclist.'

If mountains are your thing, the region is not short of them and all the ranges are much quieter than the tourist trap of Snowdon. The dramatic Carneddau contain some of the highest peaks in the country and enclose lakes such as Llyn Cowlyd and Llyn Eigiau and the 120ft (37m) drop of the Aber Falls.

From the summit of Moel Siabod, the highest peak in the Moelwynion range, it is possible to see 13 of the 14 highest peaks in Wales – weather permitting – without turning your head. Cnicht is known as the 'Matterhorn of Wales' because of its shape when seen from the south-west. The Moelwynion, a cluster of mountains in central Snowdonia, runs from Porthmadog on the Irish sea to Betws-y-Coed and Capel Curig, officially the wettest place in Wales. Betws-y-Coed has hundreds of miles of local routes, many of the challenging variety, in nearby Gwydyr Forest.

The northern end of the Rhinogydd mountain range is rocky and heather-clad while the southern end has a gentler grassy profile. In central Snowdonia is a large expanse of moorland and blanket bog known as The Migneint. Trails and bridleways are highlighted in Ordnance Survey maps.

In the south of the park is the 10-mile (16km) Mawddach Trail, a traffic-free, relatively flat, unspoilt estuary trail that runs between Dolgellau and Barmouth. The Mawddach Estuary was carved out during the last Ice Age. It is surrounded by mountains with the 2927ft (892m) tall Cadair Idris to the south and Llethr and Diffwys to the north. Admire Cregennan Lakes en route; these are situated 800ft (243m) above sea level and offer glorious views of the Cadair Idris massif. The path, which follows the old Barmouth-to-Ruabon railway track, used to carry slate from local quarries down to the coast. John Ruskin observed that only one other route had views to compare with the one from Dolgellau to Barmouth – and that was the journey from Barmouth to Dolgellau.

The longest cycle trail in Wales, the 250-mile (402km) Lôn Las Cymru, takes you down the length of the country through the beautiful north-west, all the way from Holyhead at the tip of Anglesey, via stunning Caernarfon and Harlech castles, through Snowdonia, before dropping into mid-Wales over the Cambrian mountains, on to the Brecon Beacons, then down south and east to the capital Cardiff in Glamorgan and on to Chepstow in Gwent.

The Lôn Cambria Cycle Route bisects the country. It runs from the Victorian seaside town of Aberystwyth on the west coast in a 113-mile (182km) route. It slips over the Cambrian mountains, through the Elan valley, where Barnes Wallis secretly tested his dambusting bomb, and on over the English border to the Severn Meadows and Shrewsbury. Make sure you stop close to

ABOVE: A family cycle along the Mawddach Trail from Dolgellau to Barmouth, which combines spectacular mountain and coastal scenery.

CYCLE ROUTE

BETWS-Y-COED
Circular Route

NORTH WALES

DISTANCE: 13 MILES (21KM)   TIME: 3 HOURS

This 13-mile (21km) route provides a more challenging and strenuous ride than most other routes in this book, but with the reward of magnificent scenery including a gorge, mountains, lakes and rivers. Those tackling this route should be aware that the first 3 miles (5km) involve an overall climb of around 650ft (200m). Much of this climb is not especially steep, but cumulatively the effect of cycling uphill for this distance can be quite tiring, so using a bike with low gears is very desirable. Even with such a bike, there are two or three brief but very steep sections, which can easily be walked if your puff runs out. Once past these first 3 miles (5km), the route is less strenuous, although hilly in places.

Given the challenging nature of parts of the route you should allow 3 hours or more for the ride, depending on how often you stop along the way.

STARTING PLACES

The most convenient place to start if arriving by train is at Betws-y-Coed railway station. Those arriving by car can start at the car park near the railway station.

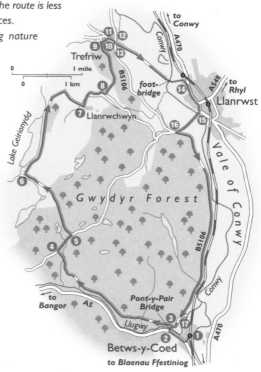

THE ROUTE

From the station entrance turn left (or right, if coming from the car park opposite) towards the main road. Turn right on to the A5 **[1]**. The short distance on the A5 is the busiest part of the route and you will need to take care along this section, especially when joining and leaving the A5. Turn right on to the narrow Pont-y-Pair bridge **[2]**. You may want to pause on the bridge to admire the rapids.

Turn left at the end of the bridge **[3]** and start the long ascent, with the River Llugwy on your left. This route offers magnificent views of the gorge with the river roaring below and Moel Siabod mountain beginning to tower above you on your left. After 2½ miles (4km) turn right at the T-junction signposted Llyn Geirionydd **[4]**. Virtually all the climbing on the ride has now been done!

Turn left after ¼ mile (0.4km) **[5]**. After a slight climb you start the descent to Lake Geirionydd, with the Creigiau Gleision ridge of mountains facing you. The road bears to the right **[6]** and takes you along the east side of the lake. There are a number of gates along the next section of road. After about 2 miles (3km) you should turn left at the T-junction signposted for Llanrhychwyn and Trefriw **[7]**. Follow this road for about ½ mile (0.8km), then turn left at the junction immediately after the red telephone kiosk **[8]**. This next section is a steep descent to the village of Trefriw, so you will need to take special care. You will ride over a bridge crossing a small river to arrive in Trefriw. After crossing the bridge you should turn right **[9]** then left **[10]**. When you reach the crossroads, turn right **[11]** and continue down to the stop sign at the main road. Take care when turning right on to the main road **[12]** which is the B5106, then cycle over the bridge and turn immediately left opposite the working Trefriw Woollen Mills **[13]**.

The road becomes a pleasant narrow track and after ¾ mile (1.2km) you will cross a footbridge, another good place to stop and admire the scenery. After the footbridge follow the road as it bears right. Llanrwst railway station should be on your left. Turn right at the A470 main road **[14]** and follow the A470 through Llanrwst as it bends left and right (with the small market square on your right). Take care turning right to cross Pont Fawr Bridge over the River Conwy **[15]**. The three-arch stone bridge was built in 1636 and is said to have been designed by Inigo Jones. Turn left after less than ½ mile (0.8km) at the B5106 signposted for Betws-y-Coed **[16]**. You may wish to make a detour to visit Gwydir Castle, a beautiful Tudor manor house that you will see as you are leaving Llanrwst.

Follow the B5106. After 3 miles (5km) enter Betws-y-Coed and turn left at Pont-y-Pair Bridge **[17]** then return to the start point using a short section of the A5.

ABOVE: The packed promenade at Aberystwyth in 1925. The town was a popular Victorian tourist resort and was once optimistically dubbed 'the Biarritz of Wales'.

Welshpool at Powis Castle, the amazing thirteenth-century fortress and its spectacular terraced gardens.

Another option from Aberystwyth is to take the 100-mile (160km) Lôn Teifi trail, which drops down along the River Teifi passing through Tregaron, where Cors Goch Caron, the largest bog in England and Wales, and the Cors Caron Nature Reserve can be found. Further along is Cenarth, which has beautiful waterfalls and a coracle museum. The route ends in Cardigan where the castle of the same name, founded in 1110 by Gilbert de Clare and a place of ongoing conflict up to the English Civil War, is currently undergoing a lengthy restoration project.

PEMBROKESHIRE

Drop south into Pembrokeshire to some of the most beautiful stretches of coastline, which comprise the UK's only predominantly coastal National Park. The coastal scenery includes rugged cliffs, sleepy fishing villages, sandy beaches, busy harbours and some of the oldest rocks to be found in the UK. North-west of St David's and south-east of Fishguard, you will find the Abereiddi Blue Lagoon, a flooded former slate quarry with a tidal channel to the sea. Further along is a coastal quarry where granite was taken down to Porthgain Harbour and loaded into boats. On the westernmost tip of Wales is St Bride's Bay with Skomer and Ramsey Island at each end. Ramsey Island, a mile (1.6km) off the coast and open to the public seven months a year, contains the largest breeding grey-seal colony in the south and birds such as the guillemot, chough, razorbill, raven and peregrine can be seen.

St David's is the smallest cathedral city in the UK. To the north-west is the beautiful sandy Whitesands Bay beach from where the dramatic headland of St David's highlights the southern extremity of Cardigan Bay.

ABOVE: A reconstruction of a Celtic Iron Age roundhouse built on original foundations at Castell Henllys, a scheduled ancient monument in Pembrokeshire.

From the granite outcrops of Carn Llidi, look down on to ancient field systems, prehistoric settlements, heathland, the cove of Porth Melgan and the great stone-chambered grave of Carrage Coetan Arthur, dating from about 4,000 BC, where, according to legend, King Arthur played a game of quoits with the tomb's capstone. Skokholm, Skomer Island and Middleholm lie off the extreme south-west tip of Pembrokeshire.

The Celtic Trail West has two routes out of Fishguard, the site of the last French invasion of British soil in 1797, both of which run to Carmarthen. One follows the coast through the Pembrokeshire National Park, the other goes inland, but both can be broken down into small sections and there is plenty to see. Plus there are numerous short individual rides, such as the 9-mile (14km) Brunel Trail, which runs from Haverfordwest through Westfield Pill Nature Reserve and on to Neyland on the northern bank of the River Cleddau. Part of the ride takes you along the route of the Great Western Railway, built by Isambard Kingdom Brunel more than 150 years ago.

CYCLE ROUTE

HAVERFORDWEST
to NEYLAND
PEMBROKESHIRE

DISTANCE: 18 MILES (29KM) RETURN TRIP   TIME: 3 HOURS

This 9-mile (14km) cycle route links Haverfordwest to Brunel Quay at Neyland. It is part of the Sustrans National Cycle Network Route 4, known as the 'Celtic Trail'. Much of the route to Neyland is along purpose-built signed cycle paths linked by quiet country lanes with lovely views across open countryside. The route should take about 3 hours if you cycle the full 18 miles (29km) to Neyland and back. However, you may want to allow more time to enjoy your stops along the way, particularly at Brunel Quay.

Haverfordwest

Freeman's Way cycle path

Merlin's Brook

DENANT HILL

A4076

Johnston

to Milford Haven

A477

Rosemarket

Westfield Pill Nature Reserve

Neyland

Brunel Quay

Milford Haven

to Pembroke

A477

STARTING PLACES

There is a large car park in the centre of Haverfordwest adjacent to the start of the cycle path on Freeman's Way. You can also start from the railway station in the centre of the town (check train times).

THE ROUTE

From Haverfordwest start at the County Hall car park **[1]** and ride along Freeman's Way cycle path to Merlin's Bridge roundabout **[2]**. Cross the roundabout using the cycle crossings and head up Caradog's Well Road past

Pembrokeshire College. Turn left on to the cycle path at the bottom of the hill **[3]**. This section of cycle path takes you through the Merlin's Brook water meadows then alongside the railway line towards Johnston. As you follow the path there is a sharp left turn across the railway track **[4]** and down to a minor road where you will need to turn right **[5]**. Follow the minor road until it crosses back to the west side of the railway line again. Shortly after this you should follow the signed left turn for the cycle route as it leaves the road (opposite the Denant Hill lane junction) **[6]**. This path takes you across the railway line once more, then you reach the road where you should turn right and cycle into Johnston **[7]**.

You should follow the signed cycle route out of the village, which takes you back on to a traffic-free path once more **[8]**. This final part of the route takes you along a converted old railway path that was originally built by Isambard Kingdom Brunel 150 years ago. The path crosses under and over a couple of minor roads near Rosemarket **[9] [10]** and through the Westfield Pill Nature Reserve, where many birds and rare plants can be seen, before passing under the A477 bridge **[11]**. The cycle route ends when you arrive at Brunel Quay, Neyland **[12]**. Neyland was a railway boom town created by Isambard Kingdom Brunel; the terminus for the South Wales Railway was built here. Links could be made with ferries to Ireland and steamships to Portugal and Brazil. The line was closed in the 1960s courtesy of Dr Beeching, but a statue to Brunel has been erected and the old terminus has been transformed into a busy marina. Here you can take a break to enjoy some well-earned refreshments before embarking on the return journey to Haverfordwest.

ABOVE: A small boy tricycles along part of the Brunel Cycle Path, which links Haverfordwest and Brunel Quay.

On the northern side of the national park lie the Preseli Hills, where the Preseli Blue stones of Stonehenge originated. This area and the rocky peak of Pen Beri, Garn Fawr and Carn Llidi, and the moorland on Carningli, are exposed and mountainous, but you'll also find the lush green valleys, such as Gwaun Valley, at the heart of bluestone country, where you can see buzzards, herons, kingfishers and otters.

Moving around the southern coast from St David's there is the Milford Haven Waterway, where the Daugleddau Estuary feeds into a deep natural harbour, and where you can see the limestone cliffs and plateau that make up the Castlemartin Peninsula, the tourist resorts of Tenby and Saundersfoot and the Bosherston Lakes. The Stackpole Estate is situated in the south of the Pembrokeshire National Park between the villages of Stackpole and Bosherston. It provides important coastal and freshwater habitats for a diverse array of wildlife and cycle routes run through it. Halfway down the cliffs at St Govan's Head, not far from Stackpole, is the tiny sixth-century hermit's chapel of St Govan, which is only accessible by steep steps. Stackpole Quay is a tiny working harbour and from here it is possible to walk along the cliffs, via a steep staircase,

ABOVE: The walled seaside town of Tenby pictured in 1905. Tenby was a popular seaside health resort during the nineteenth and early twentieth century.

to sandy Barafundle Bay Beach, which is backed by dunes and woods. To the north-east of Stackpole Quay is Trewent Point with numerous caves and arches. Briercliffe describes this area as, 'one of the grandest stretches of coast in Britain'.

Continue along the Celtic Trail West through Pembrokeshire along the wooded valleys behind sandy Amroth Beach and north of Laugharne, where Dylan Thomas lived, on up to Carmarthen, where it is alleged the great wizard Merlin was born. The Celtic Trail West continues in another loop, one side following the coast to Swansea, the other running inland through some stunning, sparsely populated countryside. If you take this route, divert up to Trapp and see the ruin of Carreg Cennen Castle, which withstood a siege by Owain Glyndŵr (c.1534–c.1416) – the last Welshman to hold the title of Prince of Wales – during his lengthy but unsuccessful rebellion against English rule.

THE GOWER PENINSULA

The Celtic Trail runs past the start of the Gower Peninsula and there are no designated cycle routes through it. However, this area is well worth a diversion from the main track, though it will be preferable to avoid the school summer-holiday period and bank-holiday weekends, as the small roads can get very busy. The Gower Peninsula was the first part of the United Kingdom to be designated an Area of Outstanding Natural Beauty back in 1965. It measures just 20 miles (32km) in length and 5 miles (8km) in width, yet contains some of the longest sandy beaches you could hope to see and has glorious sand dunes.

The coastline around the peninsula contains both rocky and sandy bays, such as Langland, Three Cliffs and the larger beaches of Port Eynon, Rhossili and Oxwich Bay. Langland is reputed to be one of the best surfing bays in Wales. Three Cliffs Bay, as its name suggests, is surrounded by three beautiful limestone cliffs, 66ft (20m) tall and popular with rock climbers. Wild horses run along the beach and the adjoining fields. Rhossili is on the south-western tip of the Gower Peninsula and an ideal location to enjoy the wildlife, unspoilt cliffs, beaches and archaeology. The beach is a 3-mile (5km) stretch of sand, popular with surfers. Worm's Head, a National Nature Reserve, is at the south-western tip of the Gower Peninsula and can only be reached by crossing a causeway at low tide. As its name suggests, the cliffs resemble the humps of a giant sea serpent snaking out into the sea. Many of the peninsula's pub menus offer a superb range of fish dishes, freshly caught off the coast.

ABOVE: The green cliffs edge sections of Rhossili Bay, a popular surfing beach on the Gower Peninsula.

The Celtic Trail East meets the Celtic Trail West at Swansea. It offers 308 miles (495km) of largely traffic-free cycling and runs through to Chepstow and the Severn, 'the gateway to Wales'. It links with many other cycling trails and from this route you can move up on to the Brecon Beacons, to Abergavenny or head up to Monmouth and Hereford. It runs cross-country through what was once the industrial heartland of Wales; one loop takes you into the valleys, the other takes a more direct line; both meet at Pontypridd. From there you can drop down to Cardiff, or move up to explore the beauty of the Brecon Beacons National Park via the 55-mile (88km) Taff Trail, which runs from Cardiff Bay up to Brecon. Large chunks of this trail are traffic free and run along old railway lines, tramways and towpaths.

THE BRECON BEACONS

The Beacons are a range of sandstone mountains in the south-east of Wales with nigh on 3,000 peaks formed by glacial action. The English name was given as a result of the Welsh practice of lighting fires – beacons – on the summits to warn of attacks by the English. This spectacular wilderness encompasses farmland, moorland, forestry plantations, caves, waterfalls, gorges, canals and a reservoir.

The Brecon Beacons National Park extends to about 519 square miles (1,344 sq km). It runs from Hay-on-Wye near the English border to Llandeilo in the west, and takes in the Black Mountains in the east, the Brecon Beacons in the centre and Black Mountain in the west. The highest mountain in the Brecon Beacons is the 2907ft (886m) high Pen y Fan. The summit can be reached in just under an hour's walk in good weather. Llangorse Lake, the second largest natural lake in Wales, has a 5-mile (8km) circumference. Legend has it that a town is buried under the waters and that church bells can be heard ringing during stormy weather. The Henrhyd Falls on Nant Llech is the highest waterfall in Wales with an unbroken fall of 90ft (27m); it drops off the Farewell Rock into a wooded gorge and is one of a series of waterfalls produced by steep-sided gorges. Sugar Loaf Mountain reaches 1,955ft (596m) in height and has a conical top from which it is possible to see the Bristol Channel and the Malvern Hills on a clear day.

To the south-west of the Brecon Beacons is an outcrop of limestone characterized by gorges, caves, swallow-holes and waterfalls, as the water from the Beacons finds its way to lower ground. Near Ystradfellte you will find Porth yr Ogof (Mouth of the Cave), the biggest cave entrance in Wales, which has the River Mellte flowing through it. It measures 1.4 miles (2.25km) in length and presents many challenges for cavers. Ogof Ffynnon Ddu (Cave of the Black Spring) is the deepest cave in the UK and the

ABOVE: A cyclist powers along the Taff Trail cycle route with the mountain Waun Rydd in the Brecon Beacon range in the distance.

second longest cave in Wales; it measures an impressive 1,010ft (308m) in depth and 30 miles (48km) in length. The area is known as Gwlad Rhaiadr or Waterfall Country and there are walks to see some of the most beautiful falls in the area; it can be wet and slippery, so sensible shoes with good grips are essential. The major falls are Sgwd Clun Gwyn (White Meadow Falls), the 50ft (15m) Sgwd-yr-Eira (Waterfall of Snow), which has a path running behind the water and Sgwd Gwladys (Lady Falls), though there are numerous other smaller falls to see as well.

There are 10 designated cycle routes within the National Park and these range from family-orientated routes to two-day tours of the mountains and valleys of the Black Mountains. There are many quiet country lanes and cycling in this area has much to commend it. There are also 16 designated mountain-bike routes.

THE WELSH BORDERS' BLUE REMEMBERED HILLS

'For Harold Briercliffe, this route was something for the more discriminating cyclist. Beautiful, inspirational, but not easy.'

CLARE BALDING

Harold Briercliffe was a cyclist who appreciated wild and rugged countryside and relished a challenge. Of the Welsh Marches he observed: 'The character of the area has been marked since early prehistoric times by the presence of two great rivers, the Severn and the Wye. It is a border district, a debatable land, and as such is reminiscent in its scenery and associations of the Scottish Borders.'

Our journey begins in West Shropshire. Harold instructs the reader to 'climb a short hill to Aston-on-Clun where the Bride's Tree, at another crossroads, is decorated afresh every May 29 to commemorate a lady who gave a bequest to the poor of the village.' This ritual, once common in villages across the country, is now scarcely practised and it is thought there are only a handful of bride's trees (Arbor trees) still in existence. At Aston-on-Clun a black poplar is still dressed with cloth annually; the flags remain on the tree throughout the year.

LEFT: Clare Balding takes a moment to check details of Harold Briercliffe's 1946 journey through the Welsh Borders.

WELSH BORDERS

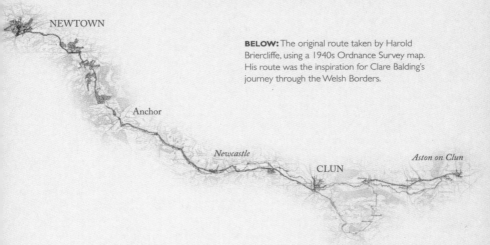

NEWTOWN

Anchor

Newcastle

CLUN

Aston on Clun

BELOW: The original route taken by Harold Briercliffe, using a 1940s Ordnance Survey map. His route was the inspiration for Clare Balding's journey through the Welsh Borders.

THE BRIDE'S TREE

The origins of the Bride's Tree ceremony are obscure. It may be that rags were tied to the tree in the hope that wishes would be granted, or it may originate from the restoration of the monarchy in 1660, when Charles II reinstated the national tree-dressing holiday that Cromwell had suppressed. In 1786 John Marston, a local landowner, married Mary Carter; their carriage stopped in the middle of Aston and the couple were so taken by the decoration of the tree that they gave the village an endowment to ensure that

RIGHT: Clare Balding sits under the Bride Tree with Rosie Evans discussing the ancient custom of tree dressing.

the tree was always decorated on the same day. One hundred and sixty five years later the estate was auctioned off (relics can be seen at the local pub, the Kangaroo Inn) around the time that Harold Briercliffe visited, but the ceremony has persisted without the endowment. The current tree is a cutting from the original, which was toppled by a storm in 1995.

HOUSMAN COUNTRY

The journey continues through wooded hilltops and the undulating villages of Little Brampton, Purslow and Clunton. Briercliffe recalls the rhyme:

> Clunton and Clunbury,
> Clungford and Clun,
> Are the quietest places,
> Under the Sun.

This ditty, used by A.E Housman in *A Shropshire Lad*, leads Briercliffe's to make one of his deliciously dry asides: 'A rhyme not without reason, for this part of West Shropshire is remarkably unsophisticated, despite its many attractions.' Housman's cycle of poems is the best-known literary work on the county, though ironically *A Shropshire Lad* was substantially written before he visited the area. Nevertheless, Housman's devotees still make pilgrimages to the places he immortalized in his poems and he remains linked to the county; his ashes were buried against the north wall of St Laurence's church in Ludlow.

> Into my heart an air that kills
> From you far country blows:
> What are those blue remembered hills,
> What spires, what farms are those?
>
> That is the land of lost content,
> I see it shining plain,
> The happy highways where I went
> And cannot come again.
>
> 'A Shropshire Lad' (1896)

At Clunton one can see the wild and stirring uplands to which Harold repeatedly refers. The vast charcoal tract of forestry land known as the Black Hill was immortalized by novelist and travel writer Bruce Chatwin, who was also looking for 'this mythical beast, the place to write in'. He arrived here in March 1979 in a battered old Citroën Deux Chevaux with a bicycle strapped to its roof and left with the makings of his masterpiece, *On The Black Hill*. Though Chatwin may have written sections of the book elsewhere, he certainly told George Melly that chunks of it had been written at the jazz singer's Welsh bolt-hole, Scethrog.

CROSSING CLUN

Clun is a small town that evolved on a hill on either side of the River Clun. Briercliffe describes it as, 'a decayed borough, whose charter was granted by Edward II, but lost in 1886. The village is a natural centre for the wide and varied region known as the Clun Forest. A Norman castle lies to the west, and is said to be the original of La Garde Doloureuse of Scott's *Betrothed*.' It is now a picturesque ruin.

Harold Briercliffe had an uncanny understanding of the particular charm and poignant historical detail that the touring cyclist uncovers. A quick visit to the churchyard at Clun reveals a 2,000-year-old yew tree, a memorial to the

BELOW: Clare Balding cycles over the famous fourteenth-century bridge at Clun on the Welsh borders route.

ABOVE: Sheep on the way to market from Clun in the 1950s. The town is on an age-old drove road that has always seen livestock on the move.

playwright John Osborne and his wife, and a tragic gravestone that details the death of seven brothers and sisters in 1811, within three weeks of each other.

Clun is thought to be one of the most ancient settlements in the country and is sited on a drove road where flocks of sheep and herds of cattle and horses were taken to markets in the Midlands. A fourteenth-century bridge divides the town in two, with the ancient Saxon part on the south and the 'newer' Norman town in the north. It gave rise to the saying 'whoever crosses Clun Bridge comes back sharper than they went.' The bridge has alcoves for pedestrians to squeeze into to avoid being trampled by livestock.

The Trinity Hospital Almshouses were built in 1614 by the Earl of Northampton to support 12 men of good character who had laboured on the land. Briercliffe came across them in his travels: 'The early seventeenth-century costume worn by certain elderly men in the town signifies that they are almsmen of Trinity Hospital.' The almshouses still provide accommodation for locals, though residency is no longer limited to men only.

Harold Briercliffe would have approved of the concept of the almshouses. As a young man he was a communist, mellowing with the passing years into a committed socialist. When he was writing his books in the 1940s there was a growing connection between cycling and left-wing politics. Socialist Wheelers, as they were known, took to the bicycle as a means of enjoying the country many of them had recently fought to defend in the war. Barry Hoban, a professional cyclist in the 1960s and 1970s who completed 11 Tour de France races, knew Briercliffe: 'There is a difference between being a racing cyclist and a tourer. Harold enjoyed cycling as leisure, not as a sporting activity.'

CLARION
CYCLE CLUB

Cycling and socialism came together to form a happy union at the end of the nineteenth century. During the golden years of the cycling clubs in the 1870s and 1880s, riders pedalled out into the countryside to escape the trials of their daily grind and to refresh and invigorate themselves.

In 1887 a letter was printed in the Socialist League journal, *Commonweal* (partly founded by Pre-Raphaelite artist William Morris), calling on all socialist cyclists to use their cycling trips to advance the cause of socialism by distributing pamphlets as they go. It took another seven years before this took off. Seven young men met in a church hall in Birmingham to debate how they could 'combine the pleasures of cycling with the propaganda of socialism'. Together they formed the Socialists' Cycling Club, a name that was changed in the second meeting to the Clarion Cycling Club, inspired by socialist campaigner Robert Blatchford's newspaper *The Clarion*. By the end of 1884 there were four more Clarion clubs in northern towns, but by early 1897 there were 70 clubs.

The first opportunity to spread the word came in 1894 when it was announced that 100,000 penny-edition leaflets were to be produced and distributed. Sales considerably exceeded expectations; 700,000 leaflets were sold by the end of the year and two million were sold worldwide. Tom Groom, one of the founding members, observed: 'We are not neglectful of our socialism, the frequent contrasts a cyclist gets between the beauties of nature and the dirty squalor of towns makes him more anxious than ever to abolish the present system.' Membership peaked in the summer of 1914 but fell away thereafter, but the Clarion Cycle Club is still active today. Its motto is 'Fellowship for Life'.

RIGHT: Members of the Clarion Cycling Club pedal through the centre of London on their tricycles on 1 January 1960.

BORDER DEFENCE

Leaving Clun, follow a hilly route to Offa's Dyke, a man-made defensive structure so huge it dwarves its better-known border counterpart Hadrian's Wall. Built in the eighth century by Offa, king of Mercia, it consists of a huge bank of soil that stretches for 177 miles (284km) from the Bristol Channel to the north Wales coast. Some 1200 years after its construction sections of the dyke still stand 25–30ft (7–9m) tall. It was built to keep the Welsh out of Mercia and parts still mark the border between the two countries. The sheer magnitude of the phenomenal construction, undertaken so many centuries ago, is humbling.

ABOVE: Clare Balding cycles through green border country along the Welsh side of Offa's Dyke near Newtown.

Our journey continues into Wales, where local folklore has it that it was customary for the English to cut off the ears of every Welshman found to the east of the Dyke and for the Welsh to hang every Englishman they found to the west. Harold Briercliffe highlighted the scenic appeal of the area: 'Those who prefer wild and lonely upland travelling will find in Central Wales an attraction that cannot be found in England and Wales without going to North Yorkshire or Northumberland. There are many miles of hill roads and paths that will enthral the adventurous wheelman when he first makes their acquaintance.'

Cycling away from Offa's Dyke, stop off at the Anchor Inn, which is just 1,312ft (400m) from Wales and is the second highest inn in Shropshire. Harold describes it as, 'an old-fashioned hostelry in the wilds of the Clun Forest'. In days gone by, Welsh farmers brought their cattle here and handed them over to drovers who would take them to English markets. Coast down Kerry Hill into the village of Kerry in Powys. Here you can take a detour along the ancient Kerry Ridgeway, an old drover's road running through woodland, heath and moorland and last regularly used 150 years ago. It follows the ridge of the Kerry Hills to the border town of

Bishop's Castle and rarely dips below 1,000ft (300m) above sea level; the views are incredible – up to 70 miles (113km) on clear days. Either have a break from cycling and explore a length on foot, or tackle some extreme off-road riding if you have a mountain bike.

Bicycle and motorbike fanatics may want to make Newtown their final destination. The town is busy and cycling not easy; Briercliffe damns it with faint praise as 'a convenient halting place for lunch'. Woollen factories and warehouses form a prominent feature of the town on entering from the south.

A shadow factory, constructed in great secrecy in 1940, manufactured parts for Fleet Air Arm planes and employed 800 people. The companies producing these tubular-steel products had honed their skills in bicycle manufacture. Work stopped at the end of the war, but in 1946 Phillips Cycles moved to the site. Production has long since ceased in the UK, but the Phillips brand is still produced under licence in the Far East. The Shadow Factory building, with its north/west orientation designed to stop enemy bombers seeing moonlight reflected in its windows, is now home to industrial units.

ABOVE: Offa's Dyke Footpath follows the border between England and Wales and is a spectacular boundary marker between the two countries.

The rugged and beautiful landscape of the border country is not the easiest cycling terrain, but the villages, and the people that lived in them, have left an indelible mark. Here a rich and poignant seam of history is exposed in poetic, inspirational and challenging countryside.

LEFT: Harold Briercliffe's photograph of a friend cycling in Eisteddfa Gurig near Aberystwyth. He described mid-Wales as offering 'many miles of quiet cycling'.

SCOTLAND

*'For nearly three hundred miles northwards there
stretches the most rugged and vivid landscape in
Britain, a wild mountainous region'* **Harold Briercliffe**

I t doesn't matter to whom you speak, or what you read, there is apparently unanimous agreement among the cycling fraternity: touring in Scotland is about as good as it gets. It is perhaps the combination of dramatic sweeps of towering scenery, the vast expanses of water and the mile upon mile of empty road that make it so very attractive. And it is loved *despite* the notoriously wet weather – May and June are the driest months, but it can rain long and hard at any time of year. As a wag once remarked: 'If you can see the mountains it is about to rain. If you can't, it already is.'

Scotland can boast many record-breaking features. Despite being half the size of England it accounts for 80 per cent of the British coastline. It is home to the tallest mountain in the UK, Ben Nevis, which measures an impressive 4406ft (1343m). Scotland has some 790 islands, fewer than 100 of which are inhabited. The landscape is vast and nothing is ever as close as it seems, especially when you are cycling towards it.

ABOVE: A pre-1924 train advertisement for the East Coast route to Scotland via the Royal Border Bridge, which is still in use today.

The area can be divided into two distinct regions, the Lowlands and the Highlands. The Lowlands account for two thirds of the populace, with the majority living around and between the great cities of Glasgow and Edinburgh. Almost all of Scotland's industry is concentrated in the Lowlands; great stretches of the countryside and coastline are incredibly beautiful. The region is dotted with castles, both intact and in ruins, relics of conflicts and heroes past. The Border country provides a scenic mix of landscapes to suit all tastes: strenuous road climbs and flat country lanes.

It is the Highlands, the most mountainous region, and the islands that are perhaps the greatest draw. Harold Briercliffe describes it as 'the most rugged and vivid landscape in Britain'. This area accounts for about a quarter of Britain's land surface, yet it is one of the most sparsely populated areas not just in Britain, but in Europe. It was not always so; the land is littered with crumbling crofts, reminders of the land clearances of the eighteenth and nineteenth centuries. Roads can be few and far between in this area and many finish in dead ends on lonely peninsulas. The coastline is dramatic, with towering cliffs plunging into foaming seas. In this beautiful and lonely wilderness wildlife abounds; here you can see soaring birds of prey, heaving masses of seals and all manner of unusual sea birds fighting for space on rocky ledges. The mountains, though tall for the UK, are small on a global scale and cycling, even in this area, does not need to be a feat of endurance. Sheep and highland cattle roam the hillsides.

While the four island groups, the Inner Hebrides, Outer Hebrides, Orkneys and Shetland Islands, are powerful attractions, many are too far away for anything other than a dedicated visit.

THE INNER AND OUTER HEBRIDES

The Inner Hebrides, which have been described as a slice of cycling heaven, are an archipelago off the west coast. They are the closest of the Scottish islands to the mainland and the easiest to reach. Take a ferry over to the famous islands of

BELOW: A cyclist travels a remote road along Claggain Bay on the east coast of the Isle of Islay in the Inner Hebrides. **PAGE 182:** A young girl performs the Sword Dance, or Ghillie Callum.

Mull and Skye, both of which offer miles of beautiful cycling and bags of history. Visit Dunvegan Castle while on Skye to see a lock of Bonnie Prince Charlie's hair, among many other treasures. Mull, the second largest Hebridean Island, is hilly and the mountains to the north attract mountain bikers. The colourful capital Tobermory, with its boldly painted buildings, is a joy – it was the inspiration for the children's TV series *Balamory*. If you visit Mull, don't miss the opportunity to take a day trip to the island of Iona, one of Scotland's most sacred places. It is home to Iona Abbey, founded in 563 by St Colomba, where parts of the *Book of Kells*, an illuminated manuscript, were transcribed, and where many Scottish kings are buried. Staffa and the Treshnish Isles are bird reserves and make fascinating trips. Uninhabited Staffa is famous for its caves and basalt columns. Mendelssohn was inspired to write his *Hebrides Overture* – more popularly known as 'Fingal's Cave' – after he was inspired by the sound of the waves in the huge sea cave on a visit to these islands.

The Outer Hebrides, or the 'Long Island', are separated from the Inner Hebrides and the Scottish mainland by the waters of the Sea of Hebrides, the Minch and the Little Minch. Enjoy clean, sandy beaches with white sand, deep-blue or green seawater, stunning wild-flower meadows on the fertile plains and small lochs, known as lochan. There is evidence of life dating back to 3000 BC, and standing stones can be seen. The islands were under Viking and Norwegian control for centuries – it was not until The Treaty of Perth in 1266 that ownership of the Outer Hebrides and the Isle of Man was given to Scotland, though the Norwegians hung on to the Orkney and Shetland islands for a while longer. The Outer Hebrides, where the Gaelic way of life persists, offers good cycling – most islands are relatively flat, though there are hilly areas. North Harris is the principle hilly exception – some peaks here are over 2,000ft (609m).

THE ORKNEYS

The Orkneys, 65 islands in total, lie across the Pentland Firth from John o' Groats. Mainland is the largest island and from here it is possible to reach South Ronaldsay and Burra via causeways. The roads are quiet, the scenery beautiful and the terrain not too demanding. There are Neolithic villages, of which the finest example is Skara Brae, a World Heritage Site, burial tombs and standing stone circles. Ferries run from Aberdeen and also from Scrabster, near John o' Groats.

The Shetlands are the furthest away, with ferries taking 12–13 hours to get there from Aberdeen; please note that cycling here is hard work because of the wind. Briercliffe describes it as only suitable for cyclists who like 'rough stuff'.

THE HIGHLANDS

The Great Glen runs along the Great Glen Fault and separates the rocky north-west highlands from the Grampian Mountains of the central highlands further south-east. A series of five lochs interconnected by rivers runs along the line, virtually dissecting the Highlands between Inverness on the north-east coast of

ABOVE: A cyclist crosses Abhainn Shira via stepping stones, near Glen Kinglass.

the Moray Firth, and Fort William on Loch Linnhe on the south-west. The Caledonian Canal, a nineteenth-century engineering marvel, enabled boats to travel safely between the North and Irish seas along this fault without having to circumnavigate the hazardous seas of the northernmost coast of Scotland. Chunks of this now make up the 80-mile (128km) Great Glen Cycle Way. The early stages near Fort William are quite flat, but it gets hilly further along, climbing to around 984ft (300m). Spectacular views of Ben Nevis in the Grampians can be seen en route; it towers over Fort William, which is a useful touring centre for the area. It continues along the west side of Loch Ness, but north of Drumnadrochit is on-road riding. Look out for the ruins of Urquhart Castle on the south-eastern slopes of Loch Ness.

ABOVE: A cyclist crosses through Glen Coe, a U-shaped glacial valley in an area of wild, precipitous beauty.

RIGHT: A postcard from the 1930s depicts the haunts of the Loch Ness monster. The myth grew after a sighting in 1933 was reported in the local press.

West and north from Fort William is the rugged Ardnamurchan Peninsula. Here you can visit Corrachadh Mòr, which claims to be the most westerly point in mainland Britain, sitting 22 miles (36km) further west than Land's End in Cornwall. Briercliffe notes that round journeys are nearly impossible but he doesn't mind: 'The constant change of scene on the winding hilly roads makes a two-way traverse essential if the full beauty of the country is to be appreciated.'

Moving north around the coast, the scenery is magnificent and dotted with castles, such as the magical Eilean Donan Castle, built in 1220 at the meeting point of Lochs Long, Alsh and Duich and in the heart of the Kintail Forest. There are fishing villages, lochs and islands to see along with ruins such as Dun Troddon, a dry-stone Iron Age structure and the fifteenth-century Strome Castle. Head through the wilds of untamed Glen Torridon on to

BELOW: A young couple in the 1930s pause on the road to admire one of the tiny islets on the shores of Loch Eilt. The famous route links Fort William and Mallaig on the west coast.

GLENFINNAN

At the head of the Ardnamurchan Peninsula next to Loch Shiel is Glenfinnan, where on 19 August 1745 Bonnie Prince Charlie, exiled Jacobite claimant to the throne of Britain, first unfurled his father's standard with his seven followers. A line of seven beech trees and the Glenfinnan Monument, topped by a kilted highlander, commemorate the event. You can also see the Glenfinnan Viaduct, which featured in the film *Harry Potter and the Chamber of Secrets* with a blue Anglia car flying beside it.

LEFT: The monument at Glenfinnan marks the spot where Bonnie Prince Charlie raised the Royal Standard in 1745 in an attempt to restore his father, James II, to the throne. **ABOVE:** The single-track 21-arch Glenfinnan Viaduct, built between 1897 and 1901, overlooks the Glenfinnan Monument and the waters of Loch Shiel.

Kinlochewe and the National Nature Reserve at Ben Eighe, where you might see the ptarmigan, the mountain hare and the pine marten.

The Far North-West Cycle Route runs for 190 miles (306km) in nine sections, starting from the train station of Culrain and running right up to Cape Wrath before looping back. It is hilly, so you need to be relatively fit. It is also desolate – here the notion that Britain is an overcrowded island will be forgotten. There are towering cliffs, thundering waterfalls, caves, rivers, lochs and wildlife aplenty. While you are near Cape Wrath don't miss the chance to visit Handa Island Wildlife Reserve, home to one of the largest seabird colonies in north-west Europe, where you can see guillemot, razorbill, kittiwake and puffin and you may catch sight of mink whales, porpoises and dolphins out at sea. Ferries run from Tarbet six days a week from April to September.

If you want to cycle up the east side of the Highlands, take the Inverness to John o' Groats Cycle Route to John o' Groats, where ferries connect with the Orkney and Shetland Islands. Cycle through the county town of Dingwall up to the village of Lairg; visit the Falls of Shin and see wild Atlantic salmon making their way up river and leaping the waterfalls to spawn in August and September. The falls are on the River Shin, 3 miles (5km) south of Lairg. Continue north up to the seaside resort of Bettyhill, which has the Invernaver Nature Reserve nearby. Move along the coast, past the decommissioned atomic reactor at Dounreay, on to the fishing resort of Thurso and John o' Groats. 'The journey is so level and the countryside so well cultivated that the tourist might believe himself to be in parts of Kent', observed Briercliffe. Look out for the most northerly castle on mainland Britain: the Castle of Mey, purchased in 1952 by the Queen Mother and restored; it is now open to the public. At John o' Groats take in the view across the Pentland Firth from Duncansby Head.

South of the Great Glen, the Lochs and Glens Cycle Route takes you from Inverness through the Cairngorms and Loch Lomond and

ABOVE: General Wade's Military Road, built in 1731 in an effort to quell Jacobite uprisings, is now perfect for peaceful cycling.

LOCH KATRINE

THE TROSSACHS

DISTANCE: 26 MILES (42KM) RETURN TRIP   TIME: 3 HOURS

This wonderfully scenic route offers the unusual option of taking your bicycle part of the way on a steam pleasure boat; these have been operating on the loch since 1843. The loch is a reservoir that supplies Glasgow with much of its water. The route runs alongside Loch Katrine, which is located in the mountainous Trossachs region of Scotland. The track itself is generally flat and quiet and runs for 13 miles (21km) between Trossachs Pier and Stronachlachar. The prolific Scottish novelist and poet Sir Walter Scott used many identifiable features from around Loch Katrine in 'The Lady of the Lake', published in 1810. The infamous MacGregor clan roamed this part of the country and the famous Scottish folk hero and outlaw Rob Roy MacGregor was born at Glengyle on the edge of the loch in 1671.

During most of the year (apart from the winter months) there is an option to travel with your bike to or from Stronachlachar using the old pleasure-boat steamer, the SS Sir Walter Scott. This service sets off from Trossachs Pier during the morning, meaning that most people who only want to cycle one way travel out on the pleasure boat then cycle back from Stronachlachar. You will need to allow at least 3 hours to cycle the 26-mile (42km) round trip to Stronachlachar and

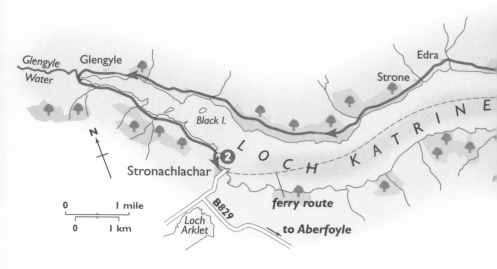

back. If you want to stop to appreciate the views and wildlife along the way you will need to allow at least half a day.

STARTING PLACES

For those wanting to travel to Loch Katrine by car, access is via a spur road off the A821 at the end of Loch Achray. The spur road winds through a narrow pass surrounded by woodland before arriving at the pier car park. There is also a seasonal bus service operating along a circular route between Callander and Aberfoyle via the Trossachs Pier and a regular bus service between Stirling and Callander.

If you don't want to travel to Loch Katrine with your bike, there are local hire facilities available at 'Katrinewheelz', part of the Trossachs Pier complex. For those wanting to explore more of the Trossachs area, cycle hire is also available in nearby Callander.

THE ROUTE

The suggested route is very straightforward. It starts at the Trossachs Pier complex **[1]** and follows the track anti-clockwise around the loch along the east and north shoreline until it reaches the pier at Stronachlachar **[2]**. There is a an abundance of wildlife in the area including red and roe deer, red kites, eagles and other birds of prey, red squirrels, foxes and even the rarer wildcat.

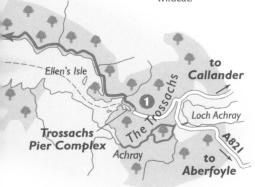

ABOVE: Loch Katrine measures 8 miles (13km) in length, making it one of the largest lochs in the Trossachs.

the Trossachs National Parks. As you leave Inverness look out across Drumossie Moor to the north-east. It was here, on 16 April 1746, that Bonnie Prince Charlie's dream of restoring the house of Stewart to the throne was finally dashed when his troops were defeated at Culloden, the final battle to take place on British soil. Cycle through the tourist towns of Aviemore and Kingussie, ascend to Strathspey Moors and on to the Drumochter Pass – the main pass between the northern and southern central Highlands. Queen Victoria is reputed to have described it as 'Scotland's Khyber Pass'. The road traffic is heavy, but cyclists move over the pass on an extremely beautiful old railway track. The route continues through the Cairngorms National Park, the largest in Britain. Remnants of original Caledonian pine forest can be found here, as can such rarities as the golden eagle, the osprey and the Scottish crossbill. To say the weather in this region is changeable is an understatement: it can be mild in March and snowy in June. Make sure you have sensible and practical clothing.

Loch Lomond and the Trossachs National Park contains diverse landscapes from tall mountains (known as munros) and moorland in the north

ABOVE: A summer evening at Loch Katrine, which is the main reservoir for Glasgow and the surrounding area. It provided the inspiration for Sir Walter Scott's famous 1810 poem 'The Lady of the Lake'.

GLENCOE
MASSACRE

Glencoe, also known as the Glen of Weeping, is perhaps the most famous glen in Scotland and runs from Rannoch Moor to Loch Leven through mountainous scenery and past Bidean nam Bian, the highest mountain in Argyll. The infamous massacre occurred in 1692, when 120 men under the command of Captain Campbell were billeted with the MacDonalds in Glencoe. The soldiers received orders that they were to slaughter their hosts in retribution for the lateness of the MacDonald clan chief in swearing an oath to King William III. On the night of 12 February, 38 clansmen were murdered and 40 women and children died of exposure after their homes were burned. A monument to the victims was erected in the village of Glencoe in 1883.

TOP: An illustration of the Glencoe Massacre, where the MacDonalds were slaughtered by the Campbells in 1692. **ABOVE:** A touring cyclist takes in the magnificent scenery at the Pass of Glencoe in 1939.

to lochs, both sea and fresh water, rivers, forests, woodlands and the rolling lowland landscapes of southern Scotland, and contains numerous cycle routes. The climb up to Glen Ogle along the old Caledonian railway route and over the viaduct is breathtaking. Stop off at Fortingall churchyard and see the ancient yew tree that is said to be 3,000 years old; whatever its actual age, it is generally held to be the oldest living tree in the UK. Move up along the valley of the

ABOVE: The former railway line at Glen Ogle makes up part of Sustrans Cycle Route 7.

River Tay and you can nip off route to visit a few whiskey distilleries to raise the spirits.

On the west side of the central Highlands is northern Argyll, a mountainous region with a wild coastline and smooth, glassy lochs that mirror the exquisite scenery. Oban is the port for the Western Isles, with ferries to Mull, Iona and Staffa. Look for the ruins of thirteenth-century Dunollie Castle, seat of the Lords of Loon. Ten miles (16km) south of Oban is Seil Island, one of the Slate Islands, which is linked to the mainland by Cleichan Bridge, designed by Telford in 1793. Quarrying for slate was taking place as early as the 1500s. Briercliffe notes: 'Inland from Oban there are a wealth of lanes and moorland tracks that will keep the thorough tourist occupied for days.'

The Crinan Canal runs from Ardrishaig on Loch Fyne for 9 miles (14km) to Crinan on the Sound of Jura. It was constructed between 1793 and 1901 to enable ships to reach the Atlantic from Loch Fyne. The entire length can be cycled, but this is not a designated route and can become slippery, so it isn't safe for children.

Over to the east side of the central Highlands and dropping around the coast from Inverness is an area fondly dubbed the 'Scottish Riviera'. The term is applied because, relatively speaking, the climate is mild and there are many sandy beaches. Inland, the fertile grass produces prime beef cows and the River Spey serves a number of distilleries. The area is also known for the quality of its salmon fishing and the rivers Don and Dee. Visible reminders of centuries of conflict appear in the form of more than 150 castles; most are concentrated in the valleys of the Dee and the Don. Look out for the high-turreted pink fancy that is Craigievar Castle, the thirteenth-century magnificence of Fyvie Castle or the splendid Braemar Castle. It was in the village of Braemar that Robert Louis Stevenson wrote the first 15 chapters of *Treasure Island*. The village is also home to the Royal Highland Gathering, which has been held annually in its present form for 200 years, but its origins go back some 700 years. The royal residence of Balmoral Castle sits 6 miles (9.6km) to the north-east.

THE SOUTHERN LOWLANDS

The Highland Boundary Fault is a geological fault line that separates the rugged Highlands of the north from the rolling hills and Lowlands of the south. It runs from Arran on the west coast to Stonehaven on the east. This fracture in the earth's crust still experiences occasional tremors. Running across the fracture and along the narrowest neck of Scotland between the Firth of Clyde and the Firth of Forth is Loch Lomond, the largest loch in Scotland, which measures 23 miles (37km) in length and between 5 miles (8km) and half a mile (0.8km) in width. There are numerous cycle routes around the loch that take you to different places, such as Balloch and Dumbarton castles. The West Loch Lomond Cycle Path is lovely and benefits from being flat and mostly off-road.

East of the loch and just south of Stirling is Bannockburn, where in 1314 Robert the Bruce defeated an English army three times the size of his own. Stirling Castle, 3 miles (5km) north, sits on Castle Hill, a volcanic crag. The first record of it dates from 1110. From it you can see for miles in all directions and it was thus of great strategic importance to anyone seeking to control central Scotland.

The western Lowlands are unspoilt and largely agricultural, with the odd notable exception: one Johnnie Walker started to blend whiskey in Kilmarnock in 1820 and a famous brand was born. The coastline along the Firth of Clyde is dotted with islands, jagged with peninsulas and inlets and glowered over by great mountains. The Isle of Arran sits in the Firth of Clyde and measures just 19 miles (30km) by 10 miles (16km), yet has a great diversity of land and seascapes. It is often called 'Scotland in miniature': the northern interior being mountainous, while the south has rolling hills and woodland. There is a 56-mile (90km) road all around the island, but you don't have to take your own machine; all types of bicycles can be hired here, including mountain bikes for anyone wanting to sample some of the rougher trails on the island. Arran is the seventh largest island in Scotland; ferries run from Brodick to Androssan. Nearby are the lovely islands of Bute, Islay and Jura, the last being the most mountainous.

North of Arran on the mainland at the top of the Kintyre Peninsula is Inveraray Castle, whose architecture shows a charming mix of baroque, Palladian and gothic influences. Further south, perched on a cliff and overlooking the Firth of Clyde and Arran Island, is Culzean Castle. It dates back to the 1400s but has been enlarged and improved by the family through the centuries. Moving south into Ayrshire, there are seaside resorts and golf courses where the hills come down to the coast and the influence of the Gulf Stream makes for a mild climate. This pastoral scene continues into quiet Galloway where ruined castles – reminders of Robert the Bruce's struggle for independence – can be seen along with ancient chapels that recall the area's role in the early days of Scottish Christianity. Further south again is Kirkcudbrightshire, a mix of the wild, the desolate, the pastoral and even the sub-tropical, notably the Logan Botanic Garden at Port Logan.

ABOVE: A 1910 postcard illustrates the same preoccupation with rain in Scotland that persists today.

Moving east along the coast of the Solway Firth towards the borders, the tide sweeps in with terrifying speed. Inland, the moorland landscape was immortalized in the film *The Thirty-Nine Steps* (1935), where chunks of the action take place around Cairnsmore of Fleet. North of here are the Galloway Hills, most of which are enclosed in the Galloway Forest Park and which is peppered with cycle routes suitable for both families and mountain bikers.

The Cheviot Hills run along the famously beautiful English–Scottish border. Littered with ruins from many conflicts, the area is known for its wool and sheep abound. Some of the most beautiful scenery in the region can be found in the valleys of Nithsdale, Annandale and Eskdale.

Trout and salmon can be found in the rivers Teviot, Yarrow and Jed, which run along the valley floor down to the Tweed. The border country is packed with ruined abbeys such as Jedburgh, Dryburgh, where Sir Walter Scott is buried, Kelso and Melrose, where the heart of Robert the Bruce is buried. The Four Abbey's Cycle Route is a 55-mile (88km) circular tour that takes in many of the historic sites of the area; most of it is on quiet roads, but there are some stretches on A-roads.

CASTLES, CASTLES, CASTLES

Castles proliferate; the triangular, moated Caerlaverock Castle and the magnificent Drumlanrig castle – where Kirkpatrick McMillan, inventor of the first pedal bicycle worked as a blacksmith – should not be missed. Appropriately, it is now home to many miles of cycle routes. Further east visit Hermitage Castle, a bleak thirteenth-century fortress owned by the Earl of Bothwell and sited south of Hawick; Jedburgh Castle, destroyed by the Scots because the

ABOVE: 'The Pink Palace', or Drumlanrig Castle, is said to be one of the finest examples of late seventeenth-century Renaissance architecture in Scotland, seen here in a painting from 1879.

CYCLE ROUTE

DUNFERMLINE *to* CLACKMANNAN

FIFE

DISTANCE: 16 MILES (26KM) RETURN TRIP   TIME: 2 HOURS

Dunfermline was the capital of Scotland until the fifteenth century and is home to many fine buildings, including Dunfermline Abbey, founded in 1128, final resting place of many Scottish kings and queens. The bones (but not the head) of Robert the Bruce are interred there. Dunfermline Palace, a royal residence from the eleventh century, adjoins the abbey; the last monarch to occupy it was Charles II. An 8-mile (13km) cycle path links Dunfermline to Clackmannan via a converted railway path that also provides connections to a series of other local and longer-distance routes. The cycle path, once part of the former Dunfermline-to-Alloa railway, is now a section of the Sustrans National Cycle Network route 76. This flat and traffic-free route is perfect for less confident cyclists, including family groups. The 16-mile (26km) round trip should take around two hours to cycle, more if you stop along the way.

STARTING PLACES

The suggested starting place is Dunfermline, although there are a series of other locations where you can join the route towards Clackmannan. If you are arriving in Dunfermline by car there is a car park on William Street, adjacent to the converted railway path. There is also the option to travel by train, in which case follow the signed, on-road cycle route from Dunfermline Town station to William Street, via Priory Lane and Pittencrieff Public Park.

THE ROUTE

Join the cycle path at the west end of the William Street car park **[1]**. Follow the path away from the town; you will pass the minor road link to Crossford **[2]** and continue on towards Oakley **[3]**. As you head towards Clackmannan you will reach a connection to the Devilla Forest cycle routes **[4]**. The forest is dominated by Scots pine and has an extensive network of paths and forest roads that are worth exploring.

As you continue on along the old railway path, the cycle route takes you on a bridge over the busy A977. Follow the cycle path towards the next bridge, which goes over the B910, but just before this bridge take a left turn off the cycle path and left again as you reach the B910 **[5]**. This minor road provides the connection to the centre of Clackmannan **[6]**. It is a relatively quiet road but you are now back on a route that carries traffic, so you will need to take care as you cycle into town. You may decide to stop for refreshments and to explore the town – take a look at the exterior of Clackmannan Tower, a five-storey tower house built of golden stone by David II in 1300 and sold to Robert the Bruce in 1359 – before retracing your route back to Dunfermline.

This is one of a number of attractive cycling routes that are being promoted as 'Kingdom of Fife Millennium Cycle Ways'.

RIGHT: A signpost for Gartmorn Dam, Scotland's oldest reservoir, on the family-friendly West Fife Cycleway and the Clackmannan Way.

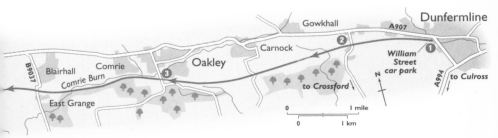

English were getting too much use out of it; and the magical Floors Castle, which was built close to Kelso by the first Duke of Roxburgh back in 1721. The Tweed Cycleway is an 89-mile (143km) route that runs from the heart of the Scottish Borders. The route starts at Biggar close to the source of the river at Tweed's Well and runs through Peebles, Melrose, Kelso and Coldstream to the coast at Berwick-upon-Tweed on the border.

On the east coast is a 20-mile (32km) wide peninsula between the Firth of Tay and the Firth of Forth with its exquisite coastline and historic buildings. Fife is home to golf. It has been played at St Andrews on the tip of the peninsula for over 500 years. The area claims to have some of the country's most comprehensive cycle routes, with 300 miles (500km) of quiet country lanes, disused railway tracks and forest tracks to use. Cycling across the Forth Road Bridge from Fife to Queensferry is said to be one of the most exhilarating experiences you can have on two wheels – and it's free. Once on the Queensferry side, take a trip to Linlithgow Palace, where Mary, Queen of Scots was born. You can follow the Round the Forth Cycle Path from Dunbar to Kirkcaldy and on to St Andrews if you want to loop all the way around this section of the coast.

Moving down the east coast into East Lothian and Berwickshire, the visitor will see fine agricultural land between the gentle Lammermuir Hills and the coast, which is home to sandy beaches, often backed by golf courses, and an ongoing fishing industry. Mighty ruined castles and fortresses litter the area; Tantallon Castle perches romantically on the edge of the cliffs just 2 miles (3km) east of North Berwick. Work started on Dirleton Castle, west of North Berwick, in the 1200s and continued over the centuries. It was the scene of many conflicts and was finally blasted beyond repair by Oliver Cromwell's cannon in 1651. The tottering ruins of Dunbar Castle sit further around the coast. This castle, once one of the most important defensive sites in Scotland, was constructed in the 1070s by the Earl of Dunbar. It came under repeated attack and was constantly being rebuilt. When the Earl of Bothwell abducted Mary, Queen of Scots he brought her here and they later returned after their marriage. Fast Castle suffered a similar fate and very little remains of this defensive stronghold – its proximity to the English border marked it out for attack. Walter Scott used the castle in his novel *The Bride of Lammermoor*, but called it Wolf's Crag. The 250-mile (402km) Border Loop Cycle Route runs in a great circle up parts of the east coast from Berwick-upon-Tweed, moving inland across the border river valleys to Peebles and Broughton, before dropping down into border country through Hawick, Jedburgh, Kelso and Coldstream.

OUTSIDERS IN THE HIGHLANDS

'The western Highlands of Scotland are truly a wilderness: mountains clad in bracken and heather, lonely glens, lochs with castles standing proud on their shores. It's seen the ravages of the Highland Clearances, when tenants were evicted to make way for sheep, and it's been invaded by soldiers and travellers who came to try and shape the land.'

CLARE BALDING

'The mountains and the sea meet sternly, and only on the narrowest of raised beaches or at the mouths of rivers are there footholds for crofts. Inland the area is cut up by deep valleys…and everywhere there are moorland and mountain and rushing peat-brown waters.' While Harold Briercliffe relished lonely and isolated beauty spots, when it comes to the Scottish Highlands he was appalled at the reasons for its desolation.

'This is hardly the place to dwell on the social injustices that led to the wholesale eviction of thousands of families from the glens that were theirs', he cautions, before wading in: 'The observation can hardly be avoided that the depopulation of the glens was, firstly, a direct result of the break-up of the feudal clan system following the failure of the rebellion of 1745 and the replacement (largely by the heads of the clans) of men by sheep and (by a later generation) of sheep by deer.' Briercliffe was of the firm opinion that nothing had been done to return this land to its rightful Highland owners.

RIGHT: Clare Balding crosses a bridge, heading for Bernera Barracks, where troops were billeted to quell Jacobite uprisings.

RATAGAN AND THE HIGHLANDS

Politics aside, Briercliffe is keen to point out that 'no means of transport is more suitable for Highland touring than the bicycle'. Our journey starts at Ratagan Youth Hostel, near Glen Shiel on the shores of Loch Duich, a hostel that Harold favoured, describing it as 'friendly'. The Scottish Youth Hostel Association, founded in 1931, opened up the countryside to cyclists, walkers and climbers who had previously struggled to find cheap, clean overnight accommodation. The Ratagan Youth Hostel, open since 1932 and described by *The Scotsman* at the time as 'Spartan-like in its simplicity', has only closed twice in the intervening years, once during the Second World War and once between 1950 and 1952 when the Forestry Commission, who owned the property, reclaimed it temporarily as housing for its workers.

THE HIGHLANDS

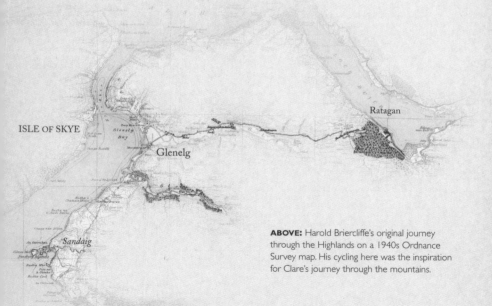

ABOVE: Harold Briercliffe's original journey through the Highlands on a 1940s Ordnance Survey map. His cycling here was the inspiration for Clare's journey through the mountains.

Ratagan is famous for its views over Loch Duich and the Five Sisters of Kintail mountain range. Legend has it that a local chieftain had seven daughters, two of whom were married to two Irish brothers. On departure they promised to return with their husbands' five brothers to marry the other sisters. The years passed with no such occurrence, so to preserve their beauty a witch turned them into graceful mountains.

ABOVE: The beautiful Five Sisters of Kintail viewed from Ratagan on the shore of Loch Duich.

The climb to Mam Ratagan, at around 1100 ft (335 m), is enough to test any cyclist. 'The gradient is mostly 1:10, steepening to 1:7 and close to the summit there is a great coil with two hairpin bends' notes Harold. Some 175 years earlier Dr Johnson and his chum James Boswell travelled along the same road: 'Going down the hill on the other side was no easy task. As Mr Johnson was a great weight, the two guides agreed he should ride the horses alternately… As he rode upon it downhill, it did not go well and he grumbled' (from Boswell's diary, 1 September 1773).

SAVING THE FORESTS

The view along this road is not the same one that Highlanders, or indeed Dr Johnson, would have enjoyed centuries earlier, due to the presence of a local invader. The Sitka spruce was first planted here in 1923, which bothered Briercliffe: 'The growth of trees being planted by the Forestry Commission prevents a continuous panorama being presented during the ascent, but at clearings the picture of Loch Duich, backed by the Sisters, is striking indeed.'

The Forestry Commission was created as a result of the difficulties Britain had in meeting demands for timber during the First World War. It was tasked with improving the country's dwindling timber resources. Sitka spruce is an attractive crop because it grows tall, straight and very fast. Campaigners want to see Scotland's natural Caledonian forest restored; this once covered vast tracts of the country but now amounts to just 1% of the total forested areas and that in 84 scattered locations. The Caledonian mix includes broadleaves as well as evergreen; all are native species, principally Scots pine, juniper, rowan, aspen and birch.

The trees that Harold complained about will have been harvested – they are cut down after 30 years of growth – and replanted. One of the principal complaints about this crop is that because of the physical planting scheme – trees are grown in tight, regimented rows – the appearance of the landscape is changed and the resultant habitat is unsuitable for the native wildlife. The good news is that the Forestry Commission is planting an increasingly diverse range of native trees in with its more productive conifers.

JACOBITE LEGACY

Our journey continues along an old military road heading west along Glenelg then northwards towards Kyle Rhea and the beautiful and isolated location of the Bernera Barracks. The barracks were built in response to the Jacobite rebellions, a series of uprisings and wars between 1688 and 1746. Troubles broke out after James II of England (VII of Scotland) was deposed in 1688 and William III acceded the throne in what is known as the Glorious Revolution.

The Scottish Highlanders supported attempts to overthrow William and, later, the German house of Hanover in a bid to restore the exiled House of Stewart to the throne.

The area around Glenelg and nearby Knoydart was a hotbed of rebellion and a Jacobite powerbase. George I dispatched Major-General Wade to inspect the country and make recommendations as to how the region could be more effectively controlled. Wade advised the construction of barracks, roads and bridges to facilitate the fast movement of troops should further conflict occur. It seems to have occurred to no one that the roads also enabled the rebels to move more swiftly.

ABOVE: Clare Balding with historian James Hunter at the Bernera Barracks, which were positioned as a key strategic crossing to Skye during the Jacobite Rebellions.

In 1719 the Jacobites became allied to the Spanish, having lost the support of the French after the Treaty of Utrecht. The construction of roads and barracks had begun, but had not been completed. In March of the same year the Spanish dispatched an army of 5,000 soldiers in 27 ships to support an invasion of England, though the force was hit by terrible storms before they could land.

In the end only two Spanish frigates landed at Loch Duich and took the beautiful castle of Eilean Donan, which came under fire from three Royal Navy ships in early May. The two sides met at Glen Shiel on the 5 June. The Jacobite army was 1,000 strong, but after three hours of fighting, the poorly equipped Jacobites dispersed and 247 Spanish soldiers were taken prisoner by the English. This was the last close engagement of English forces and foreign troops on mainland Britain.

ABOVE: A painting of Bonnie Prince Charlie hiding from George II's troops in the Scottish Highlands after his defeat at Culloden.

The Bernera Barracks, positioned at a key strategic crossing to Skye, were finally completed in 1723. They were designed to provide defence against light attack and to provide a secure base from which troops could patrol the surrounding area. The Jacobite uprisings finally came to an end after the decisive Battle of Culloden, 16 April 1746, when the army of the Young Pretender, Bonnie Prince Charlie, was routed and he was forced to flee – eventually making that famous trip to Skye and on to France. The ruins of the barracks still stand, a reminder of less peaceful times. Harold, it must be said, was not overly impressed and described the barracks as 'another ruin in Glenelg that need not detain the tourist long'.

GLENELG – A BEAUTIFUL PALINDROME

The village of Glenelg, a scattered settlement that wraps itself around Glenelg Bay, is just a short distance from the barracks. For centuries it was the main gateway between the Isle of Skye and the Scottish coast, until a new road was built to nearby Kyle of Lochalsh in 1819. A tiny ferry service still runs from Glenelg 'over the sea' to Skye, but most traffic crosses via the Skye Bridge, which was completed in 1995, finally providing a permanent link between the island and the mainland. In days gone by drovers bringing herds of cattle from the Hebrides would drive their cattle into the sea to swim to the mainland before taking them on to market.

Glenelg was the site of another of Harold's favourite youth hostels, described as 'amongst the grandest of all Scottish hostels'. Formerly the Old Ferry Inn, the building housed travellers for centuries. Dr Johnson and Boswell stayed there on their travels and Dr Johnson, whose weight had so burdened the horses earlier, proclaimed the food on offer 'inedible'. The modern youth hostel, which opened in 1945, closed in 1969 due to lack of custom and the building is now privately owned.

ABOVE: A poster for the railways from 1939 promotes the scenic delights of the Isle of Skye.

South and east from Glenelg, down a cul-de-sac, is Glen Beag and the brochs of Dun Telve and the gloriously named Dun Troddan. A broch is a dry-stone, hollow-walled, Iron Age structure built some 2,000 years ago and only found in Scotland. Briercliffe was more impressed by these structures than the barracks: 'Although in ruins, these erections are the two finest brochs on the mainland of Scotland. The former has a wall 11ft thick and 30ft in height, despite some 7ft of masonry having been taken when the Bernera Barracks

LEFT: The ancient brochs (dry-stone, hollow-walled buildings) of Glen Beag were built either as defensive structures or as status symbols.

were built'. Briercliffe's tale of the theft of the rocks from the brochs, though much repeated, is apochryphal. These towering buildings, built when the rest of Britain was living in mud huts, consist of two concentric circular walls up to 16½ft (5m) wide at their base, separated by a passageway with stairs to different levels. The rain would not have been able to penetrate the rooms in the inner circle, at the heart of which was the main living area and the all-important hearth. There would have been wooden floors at several different levels, but the ground floor may have been reserved for livestock. The building is believed to have been topped off by a conical thatched roof.

Retracing our steps back towards the coast we follow Harold's instructions: 'At the foot of Glen Beag the road swings across the Glenbeg River and mounts sharply beyond a farm to go curling around the edge of the cliffs to a height of 679 feet, whence the view southwards across the Sound of Sleat to Skye is impressive'. He observes that in the next 9-mile (14km) stretch of road there are only two farms, but he was mistaken. In fact, tucked out of sight was a third house, where naturalist and author Gavin Maxwell later lived and wrote of his friendship with an otter, described in his 1960 book *Ring of Bright Water*, which was filmed in 1969. Maxwell moved to the house with the otter, named Mijbil, which he acquired in Iraq in 1956, after life in London proved unsuitable – the otter kept biting people.

ABOVE: Clare Balding and naturalist Terry Nutkins at Gavin Maxwell's memorial. Maxwell became Nutkins' legal guardian when he lived at Lower Sandaig.

The house at Lower Sandaig (Camusfearna in the book) burned down in 1968, but a memorial to Maxwell, who died in 1969, and the otter Edal, who perished in the fire that destroyed the house, can still be found on the site. Edal's epitaph, 'Whatever joy she gave you, give back to nature', could not be more apposite. The beauty of this area is overwhelming. It witnessed rebellion and invasion, lost swathes of its own Highland people under the clearances, yet never fails to attract and welcome outsiders. The hills may be hard work, but the landscape rewards the effort tenfold.

BIBLIOGRAPHY

Briercliffe, Harold, *Cycling Touring Guides No 1: Northern England.* The English Universities Press Ltd, 1947

Briercliffe, Harold, *Cycling Touring Guides No 2: Wales.* The English Universities Press Ltd, 1947

Briercliffe, Harold, *Cycling Touring Guides No 3: Scottish Highlands.* The English Universities Press Ltd, 1948

Briercliffe, Harold, *Cycling Touring Guides No 4: South West.* The English Universities Press Ltd, 1948

Briercliffe, Harold, *Cycling Touring Guides No 5: The Midlands.* The English Universities Press Ltd, 1949

Briercliffe, Harold, *Cycling Touring Guides No 6: Southern England.* The English Universities Press Ltd, 1950

Connellan, Ian, Crowther, Nicky, Duckworth, Ian, Wells, Nicola, *Cycling Britain.* Lonely Planet, 2001

Cotton, Nick, *More Cycling without Traffic: The Midlands & Peak District.* Dial House, 2000

Cotton, Nick, *Cycling without Traffic: Southeast.* Dial House, 1994

Cotton, Nick , Grimshaw John, *Cycling in the UK.* Sustrans, 2000

Dodge, Pryor, *The Bicycle.* Flammarion, 1996

Fitzpatrick, Jim, *The Bicycle in Wartime.* Brassey's Inc, 1998

Gausden, Christa, Crane Nicholas, *The CTC Rough Guide to Cycling in Britain and Ireland.* Penguin Books Ltd, 1980

Harrell, Julie, *A Woman's Guide to Bikes and Biking.* Van der Plas Publications, 1999

Herlihy, David V., *Bicycle: The History.* Yale University Press, 2004

McGurn, James, *On Your Bicycle.* John Murray (Publishers) Ltd, 1987

Parker, Mike and Whitfield, Paul, *The Rough Guide to Wales.* Rough Guides, 2006

Ritchie, Andrew, *King of the Road.* Ten Speed Press, 1975

Salter, Paul, *Bike Britain.* An Epic Guide, 2002

Cycling Plus, *The Bicycle Book.* Weidenfeld & Nicolson, 2006

Great Britain. Lonely Planet, 1995

AA Illustrated Guide to Britain. Drive Publications, 1971

FURTHER INFORMATION

THE NATIONAL CYCLE NETWORK (SUSTRANS)

The National Cycle Network was established in 1995, through Sustrans. Working in partnership with hundreds of local authorities, and many other organisations and funders, it now provides over 12,000 miles (19,300km) of cycle routes and links. The routes are free to use and open to all.

For further information about Sustrans and more cycle routes in its network throughout the UK, visit the Sustrans website: www.sustrans.org.uk.

THE NATIONAL BYWAY

The National Byway is a series of signposted leisure cycle routes around Britain making up some 4,500 miles (7,242km) in total. It uses some of the most attractive and quiet existing country lanes and provides opportunities to visit a series of historic places of interest.

For further information about cycling in England, Wales and Scotland, visit the National Byway website: www.thenationalbyway.org.

SOUTHERN ENGLAND

For further information about cycle routes in Bedfordshire, visit the Bedfordshire County Council website: www.bedfordshire.gov.uk.

For further information about cycle routes in West Sussex, visit the County Council website: www.westsussex.gov.uk.

For further information on entering the London to Brighton Bicycle Ride, visit the British Heart Foundation website: www.bhf.org.uk/events.

SOUTH WEST ENGLAND

For further information about Cornish cycle routes and the facilities available at Elm Farm Cycle Centre, visit www.cornwallcycletrails.com.

For further information about cycle routes in Dorset, visit the County Council website: www.dorsetforyou.com.

CENTRAL ENGLAND

For further information about cycle routes in Oxfordshire, visit the County Council website: www.oxfordshire.gov.uk.

For further information about cycling routes in Lincolnshire, visit the County Council website: www.lincolnshire.gov.uk.

EASTERN ENGLAND

For further information on bicycle hire in Alton Water, visit www.altoncyclehire.co.uk

For further information on cycle routes in the Norfolk Broads, visit www.thebroadsbybike.org.uk.

WALES

For further information about other family cycle rides in Pembrokeshire, visit www.cyclepembrokeshire.com.

For information about routes in North Wales, visit www.cyclingnorthwales.co.uk.

SCOTLAND

For information about the facilities at Loch Katrine, visit www.lochkatrine.com.

For further information about Dunfermline routes, visit www.fifedirect.org.uk/fife-cycleways.

ACKNOWLEDGEMENTS

Special thanks to Laura Rawlinson and Amber Comerford for location stills photography; to all at Lion TV for their invaluable help in preparing this book, especially Steve Bailey, Alison Pinkney, Gillian Pauling and Kenny McGuinness at Lion Scotland, and to Jeremy Mills and Richard Shaw at Lion London; and Mark Jarman for his consultancy on the cycle routes. We would also like to thank the SYHA Association and Sustrans. The following groups kindly assisted with the Chichester to West Wittering Cycle Route: Chichester Harbour Conservancy, West Sussex County Council, The Heritage Lottery fund, Natural England, The Woodger Trust, Friends of Chichester Harbour.

PICTURE CREDITS

© Alamy / page 33 (bottom) © Eye Candy Images; page 33 (top) © sciencephotos; page 35 © John Terence Turner; page 43 © Nigel Housden; page 59 © Graham Uney; page 67 © Tim Tucker LRPS; page 70 © Wig Worland; page 76 and 91 © ImagesEurope; page 84 (left) © Christopher Nicholson; page 86 © The National Trust Photolibrary; page 90 © Colin Underhill; page 94 © travelib prime; page 95 © Richard Wayman; page 96 © Mark Sadlier; page 102 © Tom Mackie; page 122 © wyrdlight; page 118 © Alistair Laming; page 122 © M&N; page 126 (bottom) © Cameron Newham; page 126 (top) © Robin Chittenden; page 129 © Clynt Garnham; page 134 © Michael Sayles; page 139 © Seb Rogers; page 140 © BlueMoon Stock; page 141 © Jon Sparks; page 143 © Martin Brian Lawrence; page 144 © StockStill; page 148 © steven gillis hd9 imaging; page 153 © AA World Travel Library; page 161 and 167 © David Lyons; page 163 © greenwales; page 169 © camera lucida lifestyle; page 172 © Peter Barritt; page 173 © g bell; page 185 © Scottish Viewpoint; page 187 © Fergal MacErlean; page 188 (left) © John James; page 190 (top) © Derek Croucher; page 191 © StockShot; page 193 © Stephen Whitehorne; page 194 © Zsolt Hanczar; page 196 © John Bentley; page 201 © Gus Nicoll; page 205 © Richard Childs Photography.

© Corbis / page 138 © Hulton-Deutsch Collection; page 145 © Peter Adams.

© Getty Images / page 20 and 208 (top) © SSPL via Getty Images; page 26 (left); page 26 (right) © Popperfoto; page 29 © Wig Worland; page 37 © Philip Gatward; page 41 © Stockbyte; page 82; page 84 (right); page 88; page 109 © Ryan/Beyer; page 111 (top); page 114 and 157 © Time & Life Pictures/Getty Images; page 115; page 121; page 127 © John Constable; page 152 (bottom) © Jonathan Barry; page 179 © Evening Standard; page 181 (top) © Rob Reichenfeld.

© NTPL / page 48 © Britainonview/Rod Edwards; page 54 © Leo Mason; page 77 © John Millar.

© Mary Evans Picture Library / page 10; page 13; page 15; page 16; page 17; page 21; page 22; page 23; page 25; page 39; page 44; page 46; page 51; page 63; page 65; page 68; page 72; page 80; page 87; page 97 (bottom); page 97 (top); page 103; page 105; page 116; page 120; page 130; page 132; page 133; page 149; page 158; page 160; page 162; page 178; page 182; page 184; page 188 (right); page 189; page 190 (bottom); page 195 (bottom); page 195 (top); page 198; page 199. Page 18 and 49 © Illustrated London News Ltd/Mary Evans; page 30 © Roger Mayne/Mary Evans; page 55 © Gill Stoker/Mary Evans; page 56; page 73, 152 (top) and 166 © Francis Frith/Mary Evans; page 104 © Tom Gillmor/Mary Evans; page 170 © Grenville Collins/Mary Evans; page 207 © Douglas McCarthy/Mary Evans.

© The estate of Harold Briercliffe: pages 2, 60, 98, 123, 135, 181 (bottom)

© Lion Television Ltd: 6, 61, 62, 64, 81, 83 (top and bottom), 085, 107, 108, 110, 111 (bottom), 150, 151, 154, 155, 156, 174, 175 (top and bottom), 177, 180, 203, 204, 206, 208 (bottom), 209

INDEX